THE WHOLE YOU
Body and Mind

THE WHOLE YOU

A GUIDE TO LIFE

Body and Mind

by Jeannie Kim

AN
APPLE
PAPERBACK

SCHOLASTIC INC.

NEW YORK   TORONTO   LONDON   AUCKLAND   SYDNEY
MEXICO CITY   NEW DELHI   HONG KONG   BUENOS AIRES

None of the advice or activities in this book is intended to take the place of regular visits to your doctor. If you have concerns or questions about your health, or if you are considering any dramatic changes in your diet or level of physical activity, please consult a physician.

ISBN 0-439-40464-9

12 11 10 9 8 7 6 5 4 3 2 1   3 4 5 6 7 8/0

Printed in the U.S.A.   40

First printing, January 2003

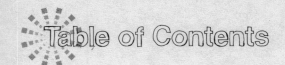
Table of Contents

 Acknowledgments

Huge thanks go out to:

David Levithan and Anica Rissi, my crack editing team.

Lisa Drayer, M.A., R.D., Director of Nutrition Services at Dietwatch.com, for her invaluable suggestions and support.

The thousands of girls (and even some guys!) who wrote to *Twist* asking for health help and body advice, and the millions more who read what I had to say about it.

The many kids who contributed their thoughts and stories to this book, including Alaina, Alex, Blair, Caitlin, Christy, Courtney, Fiona, Gina, Gretchen, Hannah, Heather, Heidi, Jenie, Jody, Jolene, Mallory, Natalie, Sarah, Sydney, and Tasha.

My fabulous friends and family, and especially Adam, who eats all of my food experiments.

The Whole You: Healthy Head to Toe

Welcome to **The Whole You!** Get ready to learn about how keeping your body and mind at their very best can lead to better things in your *whole* life.

Your body best

You probably don't think about your body all that much, as long as it gets you where you need to go and your stomach isn't rumbling with hunger pains. But understanding your body and mind and keeping them running in their best shape possible is important to keeping the whole you strong. That's because the state of your brain and bod affects every part of your life, from the way you feel about yourself to your ability to stay energized to the way you interact with other people.

In this book, we'll look at different ways to fuel your body, make it strong, feed your brain, and balance your feelings. We'll also explore what your mind and body can do, and how they fit into the bigger picture of the whole you.

What is The Whole You?

Right now, a whole world of options is opening up around you. Whether you know it or not, your life is full of amazing opportunities, and you yourself are overflowing with all kinds of potential and personality and talent that you've only just begun to discover. **The Whole You** is based on the idea that it's important to explore all of those options and **grab every chance to learn something new about the incredible, exciting whole that is you.**

Since **The Whole You** is about discovering YOU, you get to decide the path you take. That means I won't be giving you a bossy set of instructions on the best way to live your life, or a boring list of ten steps to success. You're creating *yourself* — there's no magic formula for that. I'll also never tell you that there are things wrong with you that need to be fixed. That's because every single person who reads **The Whole You** is different and cool in her or his own way.

I'm not a teacher, a psychologist, or a doctor. But as

a writer and editor for teen magazines, I've spent tons of time talking to kids from all over the world about the stuff that matters most to them. And, of course, I've been through a lot of the same kinds of struggles, questions, good times, and bad times that you're going through right now. So throughout **The Whole You**, I'll share stories from my own experiences, as well as stories from other kids. (You'll see those marked with a ✓ **"REALITY CHECK"** icon.) Everything in **The Whole You** is based on real life — not on some theory about how kids are supposed to be.

Finally, and most important, **The Whole You** is supposed to be fun. You'll find plenty of hands-on activities to get you thinking and playing — and, I hope, getting excited about exploring the whole you!

How to use this book

Like I said before, **The Whole You** is *your* journey — so you're the one who decides the way you want to use it. Every chapter of **The Whole You** is packed with activities and exercises. You can do most of the ✏ **"WRITE IT!"** exercises right in the book (or in a separate notebook, if you don't like writing in your books). ***WORK IT!*** activities are more hands-on; you might find it fun to do some of them with friends.

You don't have to do every single activity — just do the ones that appeal to you and save the rest for later if you like. You don't have to start reading at the beginning of the book and work straight through to the end, either. In fact, I encourage you to skip around — to help you do that, I've included ***LINKS*** in each chapter to point you to other chapters, other books in **The Whole You,** even Web sites and other resources that might interest you. You might feel like skimming through one chapter, then spending hours on another chapter, doing every single activity — it's up to you.

A special note on staying healthy

There's lots of information here about keeping your body and mind healthy, but this book should *never* take the place of your parents or doctor. If you're worried about how your body is working in any way, don't rely on books, magazines, or the Internet — talk to your parents, and see a real live doctor. Regular visits to your doctor are an important part of staying healthy. And never make sudden, drastic changes in what you eat or how much you exercise — always check with your doctor to make sure your body can handle the changes.

Now that we've got the serious stuff out of the way, let's dive into discovering all kinds of cool things about your mind and body! Turn the page. . . .

Chapter One

Discovering Your Body

Your body, head to toe

First things first: To keep your body healthy, it helps to *know* your body. When's the last time you really paid attention to what your eyes or arms or knees can do? The more you learn about your body and the more you explore all the things it can do, the better you can take care of it. When you know your body head to toe, you'll be more sensitive to signals that something isn't working or that you need to treat yourself better.

Plus, it's fun to get to know your body — we humans are pretty amazing creatures! Let's start at the top and work our way down. (By the way, since there's no way I can cover *everything* about *every* body part here, you might want to check out some of the resources in Appendix A to learn more.)

Eyes. Brown, blue, green, gray, black, hazel . . . No matter what color, size, or shape your eyes are, they capture light and help your brain translate it into pictures of the world around you. Your eyes give you the sense of sight, one of the ways we humans find our way through the world. Some people say that the eyes reveal a person's true self — check out the exercise on page 8 for more on eyes and emotions.

✓ ***REALITY CHECK*** "My eyes are one of my favorite parts of my body," says Gretchen. "They're blue, and in my left eye, I have a brown line. When I was in first grade someone said that meant I was special."

✴ ***WORK IT!*** How far can you see? Grab five sheets of computer or notebook paper and, using a thick black marker, draw a large symbol on each one: a circle, a star, a heart, a square, and a triangle. (If you want, you can print big letters or words instead.) Head outside or someplace where there's lots of room. Have a friend stand ten big steps away from you and hold up each sheet — can you identify the symbols? Try it at fifteen, twenty, and twenty-five steps away. How far away does your friend have to be before you can't tell the symbols apart?

☀*WORK IT!* What would life be like if you couldn't see at all? Put on a blindfold and explore your room or your house using just touch, sound, and memory. (Get a parent or friend to walk around with you to make sure you don't fall down the stairs or otherwise hurt yourself!) Can you recognize objects and people just using touch? Does your body "remember" how far it is from your room to the bathroom, or do you have to feel your way?

> **"These lovely lamps, these windows of the soul."**
> — Guillaume de Salluste du Bartas, poet

☀*WORK IT!* A lot of emotions are conveyed through your eyes. (Psychologists say you can tell the difference between a real smile and a fake one by looking at a person's eyes — with a real smile, the eyes crinkle up, but with a fake smile, the eyes don't move.) Collect a bunch of photos and pictures from magazines — try to get a variety of facial ex-

> **✂*LINKS***
> Go to *Spirit,* **Chapter 3 (The Way You Feel),** for more on expressing and recognizing different emotions.

pressions. Cover up the lower parts of the faces so you can see only the eyes. Can you guess what emotions each face is showing?

*"WORK IT!" How does your sense of sight affect the way things taste? Grab some food coloring and cook up a batch of red scrambled eggs, purple mashed potatoes, green oatmeal, or blue milk. Can you convince your friends and family to taste it?

Ears. Your ears help you hear — duh, you knew that already. But have you ever stopped to think how amazing it is that we can tell not only what is making a sound (someone talking, a bird chirping, a car driving by), but also how loud it is, what direction it's coming from, and whether or not it's moving? You can hear everything from your parents' nagging to the most beautiful music.

*"WORK IT!" Close your eyes and concentrate on the sounds around you. Even a quiet room has some noises in it, like the sound of your own

Did you know?
Your ear contains three tiny bones called the hammer, anvil, and stirrup. (The human skull is made up of twenty-nine different bones!)

breathing. How many different sounds can you identify?

☀*WORK IT!* Collect a bunch of different noisemakers — musical instruments, bells, kazoos, pans or boxes that you can bang on, and anything else you can think of. With a friend, take turns making different noises and seeing if the other person can identify the sound with their eyes closed.

> **✄*LINKS***
> **Turn to *Creativity,* Chapter 2 (Performing the Arts), for more on music and the world of sounds around you.**

☀*WORK IT!* Use a portable tape recorder to capture friends, classmates, teachers, and other folks saying the same silly sentence, like, "Spring in October is the very best flavor." Play the tape at your next sleepover — can you and your friends identify all the voices? (Be sure to write down the speakers' names as you record them so you can see if you guessed right!)

Nose. Sniff, sniff — without your nose, you'd never smell a thing. We don't use our noses as much as, say, dogs do, but your sense of smell is still pretty important. A big part of taste actually comes from smell — ever notice that when you have a bad cold, nothing tastes good? Our noses are also important because they clean and warm the air we breathe.

Did you know?
The mucus, or snot, inside your nose traps things like dust, germs, and pollen, and keeps them from getting down into your lungs. Boogers are made of dried-up mucus and all those random particles.

WRITE IT! What are some of your favorite smells? List them. They can be food smells (doughnuts, garlic, chili), nature smells (freshly cut grass, rain on a hot summer day, pine needles), people smells (clean hair, your favorite cologne), or any other kinds of smells you can think of.

Berry
Strawberry
Smoke

What are your _least_ favorite smells?

Junk
Poop

⚡"WORK IT!" Try tasting without your nose. Eat a mouthful of your favorite food while holding your nostrils shut (or wearing a nose clip). Does it taste the same to you?

Mouth. Your mouth does a lot for you every day. It takes in food (and tastes it, too!), forms the words you say, twists around to show your facial expressions, and kisses people you feel fond of. People get by without other body parts all the time, but can you imagine not having a mouth?

⚡"WORK IT!" Explore your sense of taste. Get your mom or dad or a friend to help you collect a bunch of foods with different flavors. (Some examples: salty potato chips, sweet candy, sour lemons, meaty cold cuts, tart pineapple. You can get a whole bunch of different tastes just using different kinds of fruit or different kinds of candy.) Put on a blindfold and taste the different foods. Can you tell the difference? Have your mom or dad or friend just swipe the food across your tongue, instead of putting it in your mouth — that way your guess will be based only on taste, not texture. When you're done guessing, try eating a bite of each food, one at a time, really savoring the flavor and concentrating on the different tastes in your mouth.

❀ *LINKS*
Check out Chapter 2 (Eat Up!) for more on discovering new flavors.

☀*WORK IT!* Stretch your tongue — it is a muscle, after all. See if you can stretch your tongue out and touch your nose or your chin. Compare with your friends!

Did you know? Relative to its size, your tongue is the strongest muscle in your body!

☀*WORK IT!* Try saying the alphabet while keeping your tongue pressed firmly to the roof of your mouth. Which letters are hardest to get out? Say a sentence and see if your friends can tell what you're saying.

Skin. Huh? Skin's not a body part, is it? Actually, your skin is a *very* important body part. It holds all your insides together, for one thing — imagine what a pain it would be to have to walk around trying to hold on to

Did you know? Your skin is your body's largest organ.

your liver and intestines! Not only does your skin keep your insides in, it keeps the outside out, protecting you from the sun, dirt, and infections.

☀*WORK IT!* One cool thing your skin helps you do is to feel *textures*. Walk around your house feeling different objects — the towels in the bathroom, the staircase banister, the eraser on the end of a pencil, the side of the TV, the floor or carpet, the curtains or blinds, the shoes and coats in the closet. Notice how the different surfaces feel — rough, smooth, bumpy, soft, hard, cool, warm. Can you identify any of these textures by touch only?

☀*WORK IT!* Your skin isn't a plain envelope, the same all over. There are lots of variations in the way your skin looks and feels and how sensitive it is, depending on where it is on your body. Compare the skin on different parts of your body. Notice how on some parts (like your belly) it's soft and smooth, and on other parts (like your heels) it's harder and tougher. If you have a tan, compare the skin in tanned parts to untanned parts. Is the texture different?

✳*WORK IT!* Use your fingertip to "write" letters on a friend's back, forearm, palm, and other parts of the body. Where is it easiest for your friend to figure out what you're writing? Now try rubbing different textures (a rough towel, a soft blanket) on your palm, arm, cheek, or other areas. With which body parts is it easiest to recognize the textures?

✳*WORK IT!* Close your eyes and have a friend s-l-o-w-l-y trace her finger up your forearm, starting at your wrist. Tell her to stop when you think she's reached the inside of your elbow. Look at where her finger stopped — is it where you thought it was?

Arms and hands. We use our arms all the time — to lift things, to help us balance, to give hugs, to push and throw. They rotate and bend in all directions, helping us do millions of different things.

15

Hands are also very important — our hands are what set us apart from other animals. We have what's called *opposable thumbs* — that means our thumbs can bend and rotate to meet our fingers in a pinching or grasping motion. Because of those opposable thumbs, we can write, use tools, button shirts, and do tons of other things that animals don't do.

Did you know?
Your fingernails grow faster than your toenails.

✔ ***REALITY CHECK*** "I love that my arms help me pitch fast," says Caitlin, who plays on a fast-pitch softball team. "The more I pitch, the more arm muscle I get and the harder I can throw. My arms are just about the strongest parts of my body, so they are very important to me."

✹ ***WORK IT!*** See what life would be like without your opposable thumbs. Use masking tape to tape your thumbs to the side of your forefingers, so you can't move them. (You might need help to get both hands taped up!) Try to do everyday things like eating, brushing your hair, tying your shoes, or writing a note.

✳*WORK IT!* Measure your "wingspan" — the distance from fingertip to fingertip when you have your arms stretched out to the sides. (Get someone else to help you!) How does it compare to your height?

Chest. Your chest holds your lungs and your heart, the organs that keep everything else working. They're protected by your *rib cage*, which gives your chest its shape and expands when you fill your lungs with air.

✳*WORK IT!* How big can you breathe? Use a tape measure to measure around your chest, at about the middle of your rib cage. (If you don't have a tape measure, you can use a piece of string — mark the length, then stretch it out and measure it with a ruler.) First, measure your chest when you've exhaled as far as you can — push every bit of

Did you know? When you breathe, you take in *oxygen* (along with a lot of other gases). Different altitudes have different amounts of oxygen in the air — the higher above sea level you get, the less oxygen you take in with each breath. Professional athletes often train at high altitudes to teach their bodies to use oxygen more efficiently.

breath out of your lungs. Then measure your chest when you've inhaled as much as you can — try to expand your ribs. How big is the difference?

★***WORK IT!*** Grab a friend and take turns listening to each other's heart. Use a home-made stethoscope (put one end of a paper towel or toilet paper tube to your friend's chest and put the other end to your ear), or simply put your head on her or his chest. Count how many times her heart beats in a minute. Have her do twenty jumping jacks and see how her heart rate changes.

✏***WRITE IT!*** These days, we know that the human heart is essentially a hunk of muscle that pumps blood all over the body, but people once thought it was the source of all emotions, especially love. How many expressions can you think of that use the word *heart*? (For example, eat your heart out, cross your heart, coldhearted.) Write down as many as you can, then make up some of your own.

Belly. Your belly is the area where you find most of your digestive system (stomach, intestines, pancreas, liver), as well as lots of other important organs. Like every other body part, bellies come in all different shapes and sizes.

☀*WORK IT!* What does *hunger* feel like? Create an image (draw, paint, sculpt, or collage it) that represents hunger to you.

☀*WORK IT!* Put on some music and invent your own "belly dancing" moves. Try keeping your upper body and legs still and use your belly and hips to create all the motion — forward and back, side to side, and around and around. (Start slow at first — your belly muscles might get sore really quickly!) When you've got that down, try adding leg and arm movements, too.

Legs and feet. Your legs provide the power to move your body from place to place,

Did you know? People burp or fart ten to fifteen times a day! Your digestive system constantly produces gases and you swallow a lot of air while you eat, too. All that gas has to go somewhere!

Did you know? It takes anywhere from several hours to several *days* for food to make it all the way through your digestive system.

19

while your feet support and balance you. Long, short, thick, thin, no matter what your legs look like or how big your feet are, you wouldn't be standing there without them!

✓ ***REALITY CHECK*** "I'm a dancer, so my legs are so important to me," says Blair. "There's one move I like to do with my legs called a fouetté. To do it, you have to turn on one leg and whip your other leg around straight. When you get back toward the front, you bend your leg and tap your foot against the side of your other knee. You do about five or six of these and it looks really pretty. But you've gotta have strong legs!"

▸ ***WRITE IT!*** Imagine three unusual things you could do with your legs or feet — stuff other than walking, running, kicking, or dancing. The weirder the better! (Examples: tickle someone with your toes, squeeze the juice out of an orange using your knees.)

Draw with toes

Cook with Knees

Now try one!

✳ **"WORK IT!"** How many different ways can you think of to move across your room without using your feet or legs? Try them! Then challenge your friends to a legless race.

➤ **"WRITE IT!"** Jot down five questions about the way your body works (like, "Why does skin tan?" "Why do my ears pop in an airplane?" "What makes hair grow?" "How many ribs do I have?").

_____

_____

_____

_____

_____

Now head for the library or get online and find out the answers! (You'll find some places to start looking in Appendix A.)

Changes

Your body is constantly growing and changing, every day. The most obvious change is that while you're a kid, your body tends to grow bigger and taller every year. Right around the time you hit middle school, you may go through a *growth spurt*, during which you'll gain a lot of inches and pounds all at once. When it happens and how much you grow is different for each person. (Some kids don't have a dramatic growth spurt at all.) On average, girls start their growth spurts between ages nine and twelve, while boys have theirs later, around ages eleven to fourteen. During your growth spurt, you can gain twenty or thirty pounds and five or more inches in just a couple of years!

✂ *LINKS*
Your body's getting ready to go through some other major changes in the years ahead. If you're interested in finding out more about the changes *puberty* has in store, there are tons of books out there that can clue you in. Check out Appendix A (Learn More) to get a few recommendations.

✸ *WORK IT!* When was the last time you measured how tall you are?

Make a giant ruler to track your height as you grow. Take six or seven sheets of computer paper or construction paper and tape or glue them end to end — you want to end up with a strip of paper around six feet long. Use a ruler to mark off inches and feet along the whole strip, like on the side of this page.

Decorate your height chart with drawings, photos, pictures cut out of magazines, stickers, anything you like. You can mark off the heights of random objects or people, like your favorite celebrity, your pet, the length of your musical instrument, the thickness of a stack of your schoolbooks. Add fun things like:

4 feet 6 inches = length of the Statue of Liberty's nose

3 feet = height of R2-D2 in *Star Wars*

Tape your new height chart to the wall, making sure the bottom edge touches the floor. Stand with your back against it and

-6 ↑
-5
-4
-3
-2
-1
-1 foot
-11
-10
-9
-8
-7
-6
-5
-4
-3
-2
-1

23

have someone mark off your current height. Be sure to add today's date. Mark your height at least once every few months, or whenever you feel like checking!

WRITE IT! Write a story about a girl or boy who starts out three inches tall, then grows half an inch every day — so that after a month she's eighteen inches tall, and after a year she's more than fifteen *feet* tall! What happens to her at each new height? How do her relationships with other people change?

As you grow and get older, your body's shape can change a lot, too — for one thing, some people get wider before they get taller, some get taller first, and some do it all at once. Different parts of you (like arms and legs) can grow at different rates, so you can feel clumsy and awkward for a little while as your body works things out.

You might notice that other kids are growing at a different rate from you — some are smaller, some are bigger, some are different shapes. It's natural to sometimes compare yourself to other people you know. We all do that, starting from when we're toddlers and notice that boys are different from girls, or that some people have hair that's a different color or skin that's a different shade. But since everyone changes and grows differently, it's not very useful to compare your body's shape and size to that of other people, whether it's kids you know or celebrities in magazines or movies. Take it from me, **no matter what your body looks like or acts like right now, chances are it's perfectly normal — for *you*.** Your body will keep changing all your life, so there will always be new things about your body to get to know!

☀️ **"WORK IT!"** What did the world look like when you were smaller? Spend some time moving around your house on your hands and knees or on your tummy. What's at eye level? How is your perspective on things different?

"WRITE IT!" List three things about your body that are different from two or three years ago. (They can be things your body does or things that look different.)

teeth missing

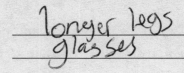

longer legs
glasses

☛*WRITE IT!* What if everybody woke up looking completely different every morning of their lives? You might be three feet tall one day and eight feet tall the next; blond on Mondays and blue-haired on Tuesdays; body parts changing shape and size from one day to the next. Write a story or poem set in this imaginary world.

Loving the body you're in

All this growing and changing can change how you feel about your body, too. Sometimes you might feel like you don't even recognize it! But you can always find things to love about your new frame, no matter what's happening to it.

You see, **loving your body isn't just about liking the way you look. It's also about valuing your body for what it does and how it feels.** After all, your body does so much more than wear clothes and look nice — it carries your brain around, plays sports, keeps you alive by breathing and pumping blood, hugs your friends, and does a million other amazing things.

When you feel confident about what your body can do, you feel better about your bod, no matter what it looks like. I've learned that firsthand. After I go for a swim or a run, I feel strong and powerful. I don't care what shape my belly is or whether I have a zit — I just feel the blood pumping and the strength of my muscles, and I feel like I have the best body in the world.

> **"If any thing is sacred, the human body is sacred."**
> — from "I Sing the Body Electric" by Walt Whitman, poet

I feel the same way when I perform on the violin. Before I get onstage, I might fuss over my hair and makeup and worry about what to wear, but when I'm playing I'm only thinking about the wonderful things my arms and hands can do, and how good it feels to make music.

✔ ***REALITY CHECK*** "I love my arms," says Mallory. "They're really strong, which helps a lot when I'm playing sports. When we lift weights at school, I always feel so proud of myself because I can lift so much more than the other girls in my class. It makes me feel awesome!"

> **⊹*LINKS***
> To explore some of the things *your* body can do, turn to Chapter 3 (Working It).

WRITE IT! Write down three things your body does that you're proud of, and why. (Do you have strong legs that help you score goals on the soccer field? Are you flexible enough to touch your toes or do back bends? Do you have super-sharp eyesight? Are your hands good at fixing things? Can you dance? Do you love riding your bike, climbing trees, swimming underwater, diving off the high dive, doing cartwheels, snowboarding, playing drums?)

1. _Strong arms_

2. _Neat handwrighting_

3. _long legs_

WRITE IT! What are some things that make your body feel good — energized, powerful, strong, or free? List five. (Some examples: running as fast as you can, swimming underwater the whole length of the pool, doing crazy cartwheels across the lawn, cannonballing off the diving board, doing a handstand, eating a perfect apple when you're really hungry, laughing until your stomach hurts, playing your favorite song on the saxophone, giving your little sister a piggyback ride.)

❖ *LINKS*
Turn to *Spirit,* **Chapter 5** (Accepting Yourself — and Everyone Else), for more on loving the whole you, just as you are.

1. _____ *running fast* _____

2. _____ *giving horse Rides on my back* _____

3. _____

4. _____

5. _____

Do one of those things today!

Body bummers

Sometimes people don't feel so great about their bodies. They feel like they look bad or they worry that other people think they look bad, or that they don't measure up to people around them or celebs they see on TV.

Being bummed about your body is bad for lots of reasons. First of all, disliking *anything* about yourself feels lousy, no matter what. Second, when you obsess

✿❖✿*LINKS*
Check out
Spirit, Chapter 1
("Who Am I?"),
for more on
how the whole
you is more
than just a
collection of
parts.

about something you don't like about your body (or *any* little thing you don't like about yourself), you're acting like the only thing that matters about the whole you is that one little thing — your toes, say, or your hair, or your butt. You are more than just your toes!

Finally, feeling bad about your body just takes away from time you could be spending exploring the whole *rest* of you. Instead of worrying about the size and shape of your body parts, you could have spent all that energy thinking about your history test, the great performance you're going to give in the school play, or the touchdown you're going to make next week.

You don't have to look like a movie star to love your bod — you just have to treat yourself like a movie star! To

"I used to not like my mole. But I think once I lived with it and accepted it, I think that helped me accept myself."
— Cindy Crawford, model

do that, **focus on things that make you feel good about yourself,** like the way you feel when you're laughing really hard or when you score a goal. Don't compare yourself to other people — everybody is different and special and lovable in a unique way. Instead of criticizing any parts of you that you're not crazy about, try to be nice to them — who knows, maybe you'll even learn to love them!

✓ ***REALITY CHECK*** Even little things can make you feel awesome about your body. "I feel great when a really cool outfit at the mall fits me just right," says Sarah.

Mallory focuses on how her body feels from the inside: "Knowing that I'm in good shape and living a healthy life makes me feel good about my body," she says.

"I used to be really self-conscious about the way I looked," says Jody. "But I finally decided that I didn't care what people thought of me. If they didn't like me for who I was, then, oh well. Anytime I don't feel good about the way I look, I just tell myself that I'm not out to impress anyone but myself."

☀*WORK IT!* Make a pro-body pact with a friend. Promise each other that if one of you says something negative about her body, the other will give her a compliment and help her stop trashing herself.

☀*WORK IT!* Feeling like you could use a body boost? Grab the list of things that make your body feel good (the one you wrote in the previous section). (If you haven't done it yet, make one now!) Do something that's on your list, right now!

Chapter Two
Eat Up!

Play with your food

"Eat your veggies," your parents are always nagging. "Drink your milk." "Finish your spinach or you won't get dessert." "Don't play with your food." Ugh. How is it that parents can manage to make food seem like such a chore? The fact is, **eating should be fun**. There are so many tastes and smells and textures, there's almost no limit to the variety of food experiences you can have.

Most of us tend to eat more or less the same things again and again, usually just because we like those things, and also because no one knows how to cook *everything* (or has the time!). There was a time in my life when I would have happily eaten nothing but my mom's pork dumplings day in and day out — forever. But part of the fun of eating is branching out from your regular choices and discovering cool new flavors. Who knows — maybe one of those unfamiliar tastes could become a new favorite!

✓ *"REALITY CHECK"* Everybody's got favorite foods. Heather goes for french fries and cold chicken noodle soup. Sarah loves fruits and vegetables: "They make me feel energized." Tasha loves fruit, too: "It tastes good, and when I eat it I feel like I did something right." Sydney says, "My favorite foods are chocolate, because it's nature's antidepressant, and doughnuts, because they kick butt!" Gina raves, "I like ice cream, macaroni and cheese, pizza, popcorn, and, well, junk food!"

It's fun to try new stuff, even if you're not usually very adventurous about food. "I'm not really into trying new things, but last year in Florida I tried alligator for the first time and I loved it!" says Courtney. "I even brought some home!"

"WRITE IT!" What are your five favorite foods?

1. _____ Pasta _____

2. _Oreo_
3. _M & M_
4. _grilled chee_
5. _chicken taco_

★*WRITE IT!* Pick one of your favorite foods. Imagine that you have to describe the way it tastes to someone who has never tried it. How would you explain the flavor, texture, smell, temperature?

✹*WORK IT!* On the next few pages, you'll find a long list of different foods and flavors. (It's in alphabetical order, but I picked stuff at random, so there are thousands of other flavors out there that aren't listed here!) Go through the list and check off every one you've ever tried. You might check off a lot, or you might check off just a few. Check with your parents if you're not sure about something or don't recognize the name — some flavors, like sage or curry, you might have tried but just didn't know their names.

almonds ✓

anchovies

angel food cake

anise ✓

apples ✓

apricots

artichokes

arugula

asparagus

avocados ✓

bacon ✓

bananas ✓

barbecue sauce

barley

basil

bean sprouts

beef

beets

biscuits

black beans

blackberries ✓

blueberries ✓

broccoli ✓

Brussels sprouts

cabbage ✓

caramel ✓

cardamom ✓

carrots ✓

cashews ✓

cauliflower ✓

celery ✗ NoT Yet

cheddar cheese ✓

cherries

chicken

chickpeas ✓

chili

chocolate ✓

chorizo

chutney

cilantro ✓

cinnamon ✓

clams

coconut

collard greens

corn ✓

cottage cheese

couscous ✓

cucumbers ✓

curry

custard

crab

duck

eggs

eggplant

falafel

fennel

figs ✓

french fries ✓

garlic ✓

ginger

goat cheese

gorgonzola cheese ✓

grapefruit ✓

green beans ✓

grits

guacamole

hoisin sauce

honey

hummus ✓

jalapeños

ketchup ✓

kimchi

kiwi

lamb

lemons

lentils

lettuce

lima beans

limes

lobster

macadamia

   nuts

mango

maple syrup

mayonnaise

mint

miso

mozzarella

   cheese ✓

muffins ✓

mushrooms

mustard

nachos

nectarines

noodles ✓

oatmeal

okra

olives

onions

oregano

oysters ✓

pancakes ✓

papaya

Parmesan

   cheese ✓

peaches

peanuts ✓

pears

peas ✓

pecans

pickles

pineapple

pistachio nuts

pita

plantains

plum

pomegranate ✓

poppy seeds

pork

potatoes ✓

pudding ✓

pumpkin

raspberries

red peppers

rhubarb

ribs

rice (white,

   brown, wild) ✓

rosemary

rye bread

saffron

sage

salmon

salsa

scallions

seaweed ✓

sesame

shrimp

soy sauce

sourdough

   bread ✓

spinach

squid

strawberries ✓   tofu   waffles ✓

sunflower seeds   tomatoes   walnuts

sushi   tuna   wasabi ✓

sweet potatoes   turkey   watermelon ✓

tahini   turnips   whipped cream

teriyaki   vanilla ✓   wontons

thyme   vinegar   zucchini

Pick five things from this list that you *haven't* tried. Ask your parents if can you try each of them sometime this month, either at home or at a restaurant.

WRITE IT! Can you think of five things you've tasted that *aren't* on this list?

_____

_____

_____

_____

_____

WORK IT! Experiment with different flavor combos by inventing your own smoothie recipes. To make a basic smoothie, you need:

- a blender (ask permission first)
- around 2 cups of fresh or frozen fruit. Use any kind you like and as many kinds as you like!
- 1-2 cups milk or yogurt. If you don't like dairy, you can use fruit juice instead for a less creamy smoothie. (I like to use vanilla soy milk.)
- ice (if you use frozen fruit, skip the ice)

Cut the fruit into little pieces and remove stems and seeds. Put it in a blender, pour in milk or yogurt, toss in a few ice cubes or a handful of crushed ice, and puree until smooth. (You may have to experiment with the amounts of ice and milk or yogurt until you find a consistency you like.) Add a little honey if you think it needs sweetening, or try other flavors such as cinnamon, nutmeg, chocolate, peanut butter, or whatever else you can think of. If you're using yogurt, try vanilla or fruit yogurt instead of plain to add another flavor dimension. Play around with different combinations and concoct your own special smoothies. How about a Berry Explosion (strawberries, blueberries, raspberries, and blackberries), a Peanut Butter Banana Split (bananas, vanilla yogurt, peanut butter, and chocolate syrup), or a Tropical Twist (pineapple juice, mango, banana, and papaya)?

WORK IT! With your parents, pick out a cookbook devoted to a specific kind of cuisine, such as Chinese, Indian, Italian, Mexican, Japanese, Thai, German, Cuban, Greek, Korean — or whatever catches your eye. With an adult's help, try out a recipe for a dish you've never had before. You can also browse through recipe Web sites to find ideas. (Try searching for a specific ingredient, like one of the things you'd like to try from the list on pages 36–38.)

> ***LINKS***
> **Check out Appendix A (Learn More) for cookbooks and Web sites that can help inspire you.** *Creativity*, **Chapter 4 (Create Something!), has more on getting creative in the kitchen.**

WORK IT! Field trip time! Does your town have a market or grocery store devoted to certain ethnic foods? Most big cities have at least one Asian market; yours might have a Spanish market, a Jewish specialty food store, an Indian grocery, a Polish meat market, a French bakery, or other kinds of stores, depending on where people in your area are from. (Ask your parents or check the phone book if you're not sure. If you're positive your area doesn't have anything like that, see if your local grocery store has an ethnic food section.) Take a trip there with an adult, and spend some time going up and down the aisles. Inhale the different smells in the air; squeeze, poke, and sniff unidentifiable packages. (This is where it's helpful to have an adult with you, so the store owner doesn't think you're just messing around!) Look at the different kinds of foods they have on sale, and take a whiff of the spices. Are there things you don't recognize? If you're feeling adventurous, ask someone at the store to recommend a snack you can sample.

✂ *LINKS*
Check out Chapter 1 (Discovering Your Body) for more on exploring taste and smell.

📢 *WRITE IT!* Pretend you're an explorer who's stumbled on a new place — a jungle, a gorgeous castle high in the mountains, even a civilization on another planet. You attend a banquet there — describe what it's like. What kinds of foods and flavors do you experience, and how do you react? How will you describe it all to the people back in your homeland?

"WRITE IT!" Lots of families have traditions that center around food. For example, in my house, dumpling-making day was always a special occasion. Two or three times a year, my mom mixed up a huge vat of filling, and the whole family would sit around the kitchen table folding the filling into wrappers to make dumplings, or *mandoo*, while we talked and told stories. My brother and I always competed to see who could eat more dumplings at one sitting (I think the record was twenty-five). Do you have any family food traditions? Maybe there's a special dish that's always served at holiday dinners, or maybe you have a tradition of going out for pizza after a big game, or hitting the fried dough booth at the state fair every summer. Describe your family's food tradition — how did it get started? How long has it been going on? What makes it special to you?

Cooking makes food more fun, too. It's exciting to try making new things and it's really satisfying to eat something you made yourself. Cooking is also a great activity to do with someone else, like a parent, brother or sister, or your best friend, because it's creative and messy and you get to eat the results!

> ✓ ***REALITY CHECK*** "I love to cook!" says Blair. "My favorite things to make are sweets, like chocolate-chip cookies and cakes — oh, and macaroni and cheese!" Heidi likes to cook vegetables, desserts, and pasta. Courtney rocks at making breakfast: "My favorite things to cook are eggs, pancakes, bacon — simple stuff like that."

Here are a few fun food ideas — you can try them at a sleepover, birthday party, or just some boring Saturday. Be sure to get permission before you start messing around in the kitchen, and have an adult supervise or help, especially if you're using knives or the stove or oven.

☀**"WORK IT!"** Have a pizza-face contest. You'll need:

- Pita bread or large-sized English muffin halves
- Your favorite tomato sauce or pizza sauce
- Cut-up veggies: broccoli, tomatoes, olives, yellow and green squash, spinach, mushrooms, red and green peppers, onions, or whatever you like (have a grown-up supervise the chopping)
- Shredded mozzarella cheese

Each person gets one pita or muffin half. Spread the pita or muffin with tomato sauce. Then create a "face" using veggies to make the eyes, nose, mouth, hair, mustache, or whatever you're inspired to do. Vote on whose face is the silliest or the most realistic or the best self-portrait. Sprinkle a little cheese on each face, place them on a cookie sheet, and bake in an oven at 400 degrees Fahrenheit until the cheese melts and gets bubbly. (Get a grown-up to help with the oven part.) Then eat your face!

☀"WORK IT!" Bake your own birthday cake. Use a cake mix or make it from scratch, depending on your skill level, and get your friends to help. You could even make cupcakes and let all your friends decorate their own. (P.S. When you make your own cake, you can put as much frosting on it as you want!)

☀"WORK IT!" Declare one night a month "Kids Cook" night at your house. That night, you (and your siblings, if you have any) cook dinner for the adults in your house. You don't have to get all fancy — if all you can make is toast, make toast! But *you* plan the menu and make it all, from start to dessert. (You may want to have an adult in the kitchen while you cook, just for safety's sake.)

☀"WORK IT!" Get together with your parents to invent silly theme food days. Declare next Thursday "Green Day," and make all green food — pick all the other colors of marshmallows out of your Lucky Charms, have green peppers for a snack, mash your potatoes with a drop or two of green food coloring, and have pistachio or mint ice cream for dessert. Or have a "Letter of the Week" meal — every week, have one meal where everything in the meal starts with the same letter. (For example, biscuits, beef, buttered beans, and banana bread, or pickles, pork chops, potatoes, and peppermint patties.)

Feed your bod

Of course, you know that eating isn't something we do *just* for fun. Food is important for fueling your body, the way gas fuels a car. Eating right affects how you function in every way:

- **It keeps all your parts working.** The food you eat makes your eyesight sharp, helps your muscles move you around, keeps your heart pumping regularly, even strengthens your hair and nails. When you don't eat enough of the right stuff, your body has a harder time making it all work.
- **It energizes you.** You may have heard of something found in food called *calories*. That's just

another way of saying *energy*. When you don't eat enough, you don't have enough energy to get through the day.

- **It feeds your growing body.** Back in Chapter 1, I mentioned that your body is constantly growing and changing. Without the right food, it's hard for your body to build your bones, muscles, and every other part of your body.

- **It keeps you smart, creative, and alert.** When your body hasn't been fed, your brain feels it, too. Ever notice how you get cranky and can't concentrate if you're hungry? Plus, your brain needs the right stuff to function and grow, just like the rest of your body.

LINKS
Turn to Chapter 4 (Feed Your Brain) for the scoop on foods that keep your brain working.

The good news is that you don't have to go on some strict eating plan to eat right. (Besides, no one knows what the perfect eat-right plan is — there probably isn't one!) Think of it this way: **Concentrate on adding more good stuff to fuel your body.** *Don't* worry too much about cutting out all the "bad" stuff. That means you don't have to give up eating junk food or anything else you love, as long as you're eating enough good stuff as well (whew!).

To add more of the good stuff, focus on trying new things and eating lots of different foods each day. That makes it easier to have fun with your food *and* make sure you get enough energy and nutrition to get through the day. It's also a lot more fun than following some boring diet plan. Try to eat these things every day:

Fruits and vegetables. Fruits and vegetables are incredibly important. They're packed with vitamins, fiber, and other good stuff that your body needs. **People who eat more fruits and vegetables are healthier — it's a proven fact.** So eating lots of them is one of the best ways to make sure you're eating right.

It's great if you can eat at least five servings of fruits and vegetables a day. (More than five is even better!) But that doesn't mean choking down five bowls of green glop. First, a serving is actually pretty small — a medium-sized piece of fruit, a handful of raisins or berries, a small glass of fruit or vegetable juice, half a cup of cooked veggies or cut-up fruit, one cup of raw leafy vegetables or salad. So if you cut up a banana over your cereal and have a glass of orange juice at breakfast, you've already got two servings down! A fruit cup at lunch adds another serving, and so does a handful of mini carrots as an after-school snack. A side salad with dinner could be two servings or more, depending how big it is and how much other stuff you put on it. Presto — six servings!

Second, it's easy to sneak in fruits and veggies in tasty ways — how about tomato sauce on your pizza or pasta, salsa on your taco, or blueberries in your pancakes? Have fun trying lots of different ingredients (use the list of foods at the beginning of this chapter as inspiration) so you won't get bored eating the same old apples every day.

☀**"WORK IT!"** Try some of these tricks to add more fruits and veggies to your day:

- Stir fruit into your cereal or oatmeal in the morning, or toss berries on your pancakes or waffles.
- Drink fruit juice instead of soda — apple and orange, sure, but how about trying pineapple, mango, grapefruit, guava? You can even

buy carrot juice! (Look for brands that say "100% juice" on them, since a lot of "juices" are mostly sugar and water.)

- Stuff boxes of raisins or other dried fruits in your backpack to snack on during the day.

- Have a piece of fruit when you get home from school.

- Munch on carrot sticks while you watch TV (celery sticks spread with peanut butter or cream cheese are also great snacks) — ask your parents to buy the prewashed mini carrots to make it even easier.

- Have fruit-on-the-bottom yogurt.

- Make a peanut-butter and banana sandwich.

- Become a smoothie fiend — check out the smoothie how-to on page 38.

- Add grated carrots or chopped spinach when you heat up store-bought spaghetti sauce — you can't even tell they're there, and you'll get a vegetable double whammy.

- Treat yourself to one of those frozen fruit-and-juice bars, or make your own version: Fill an ice-cube tray with your favorite juice, pop a chunk of fruit in each cube, then freeze to make a fun summer snack. Invent funky combinations — how about apple juice with grapes, orange juice with blueberries, or tangerine juice with strawberries and peaches?

- Top ice cream or cake with slices of fruit.
- Get veggies on your pizza (mushrooms, peppers, broccoli, tomatoes . . .).
- Toss in frozen peas, broccoli, or other veggies when you make macaroni and cheese — you'll hardly notice them, covered in cheesy sauce.
- Put salsa on everything!
- Get lettuce and tomato on your burger or sandwich. (Don't love lettuce? Try slices of cucumber or bell peppers or raw spinach leaves.)
- Instead of cookies or candy for a sweet snack, drizzle a little chocolate syrup on slices of fruit (apples, pears, oranges, strawberries, whatever you like!).

✓ **"REALITY CHECK"** "I love applesauce," says Natalie. "It's refreshing and fills you up. If I want junk food or something like that, I'll just get a bowl of applesauce and when I'm done, I don't have that craving for junk food."

"For breakfast I always try to add fruit and sometimes yogurt to go along with my oatmeal," says Christy. Mallory tries to eat a fruit or veggie with every meal. "I eat lots of apples and carrots and green beans," she says. "And when I want a cookie, I just munch on an apple, which is twice as filling, anyway."

Heidi's a vegetarian, so vegetable dishes are some of her favorites. "I like salad a lot, and I like green beans mixed with carrots. Yum!"

✳ **"WORK IT!"** This week, try one new fruit or vegetable that you've never had before. You might get together with whoever does the cooking in your family to figure out how to add it to one of your family meals.

☀*"WORK IT!"* Keep track of how many fruit and vegetable servings you eat every day by sticking gold stars or stickers on a calendar. (Use the tips in the previous exercises to add more servings to your day.) If you get five a day for a whole week, treat yourself to a reward, like renting your favorite movie.

☀*"WORK IT!"* Eat a rainbow. Brightly colored fruits and veggies are packed with vitamins and other healthy stuff, and eating lots of different colors is a good way to make sure you're getting lots of different important nutrients. To see how you're doing, every time you eat a fruit or vegetable, draw a stripe in that color on your calendar. See if you can complete a rainbow in one week. (Think that's too easy? See if you can complete a rainbow in one *day*.) Some suggestions (can you think of more?):

Red: tomatoes/tomato sauce, strawberries, cranberries, raspberries, red bell pepper, watermelon, cherries, beets

Orange: sweet potatoes, oranges, winter squash, carrots, cantaloupe, pumpkin, mango, nectarines, papaya

Yellow: banana, yellow squash, yellow bell pepper, corn, pineapple, lemons

Green: peas, broccoli, spinach, lettuce, asparagus, avocado, honeydew melon, kiwi, green olives, Swiss chard, bok choy

Blue: blueberries, plums

Purple: eggplant, purple grapes, blackberries, raisins, figs

Grains are a major source of *carbohydrates,* the part of your daily food intake that provides the most energy for your body. Grains are part of everyday foods like bread, rice, pasta, and cereal. You can also find more unusual grains like barley or bulgur. Most kids don't have any trouble eating enough of this stuff — hello, pizza crusts, peanut butter and jelly sandwiches, and macaroni and cheese! But it's fun to add some variety in the grains you eat.

"WRITE IT!" For three days, write down all the grains you eat — breakfast cereal, granola bars, bread, rice, pasta, whatever you eat. How many different kinds of grain foods do you have on your list? Do you tend to eat a lot of the same things, like white bread or pasta?

✴*WORK IT!* Tomorrow, eat a different kind of grain at each meal. If you have cereal for breakfast, have a sandwich on rye at lunch and rice at dinner. If you have toast for breakfast, try noodles at lunch. White rice, cereal, pasta, and bread are all good options, but you can also try more exotic grains, like kasha, cous-cous, barley, bulgur, wheat berries, wild rice, and basmati rice. (Get together with whoever does the cooking at your house and plan a meal where you can try making a "new" grain.) Try *brown* grains, too — like brown rice, whole wheat tortillas, and multigrain bread. They add different flavors to your day — and they happen to contain lots more vitamins, minerals, and fiber than white rice and white flour.

Protein. Your skin, hair, muscles, and many other parts of your body are made of *protein*. That's why you need to eat foods that contain protein regularly to help your body build itself up — especially now, when you're growing. People can get protein from lots of different sources — meat, poultry (chicken and turkey), fish, and eggs, but also beans, nuts, dairy products, and soy foods like tofu or soy milk. Even grains and vegetables contain some protein!

Dairy products (like milk, cheese, and yogurt), soy, and beans have the added bonus of being good sources of *calcium*, which is important for building strong bones and teeth — especially now, when you're still growing. Try to eat three or more foods that provide calcium each day. (Other good sources of calcium include broccoli; leafy greens like spinach, collards, and turnip greens; calcium-fortified orange juice; and calcium-fortified cereal and bread.)

Most Americans eat plenty of protein, so you probably don't need to worry about it too much. But try mixing up your meals with different *kinds* of protein — have a black bean burrito or fish taco instead of beef, snack on nuts or yogurt, try tuna instead of bologna in your sandwiches, even throw sausage on your pizza instead of pepperoni. (Check out the section on vegetarianism later in this chapter for more info on getting your daily protein without meat.)

Water is so essential that we humans can survive only a couple of days without it. Every part of your body needs water to work properly, from your brain to your toes. Since you're constantly losing water through peeing, sweating, and other processes, you need to drink around six to eight glasses of water a day to replace the water you lose and keep everything running smoothly. If it's hot out or you're exercising, you need even more. Not getting enough water can make you tired, cranky, even hungry!

The good news is that you can get your daily dose of water not just by drinking plain water, but by gulping down juice or milk, having a bowl of soup, or eating fruits and vegetables (which contain lots of water). (Soda contains water, too, but it also has tons of sugar and not much other nutritious value. Juice, milk, or plain water are usually better choices.) And you don't have to drink six glasses all in a row — in fact, you probably shouldn't! Instead, try to drink a glass of something with every meal or snack — that way, you'll keep your energy level up and won't get too thirsty.

Sweets and treats. Ha! Bet you're surprised to see this here, aren't you? Of course you don't *need* them to eat healthfully, but how much fun would life be if you could never ever eat candy or ice cream or chips? Besides, if you banned your favorite snacks from your life, you'd quickly go crazy craving them!

So have sweet treats and other yummy junk food — just try to eat smaller amounts of them. (Sweets aren't the best fuel for your body because they don't contain lots of the vitamins and minerals your body needs.) Have one or two cookies instead of a handful, one scoop of ice cream instead of two, or medium fries instead of supersizing it — and really enjoy the food while you're eating it, concentrating on the yummy taste.

✓ ***REALITY CHECK*** "I watch what I eat, but I never deprive myself of french fries, ice cream, or pizza," says Christy. "I eat whatever I want, but in moderation. That way I don't crave foods that I'm not 'allowed' to have."

Going Veggie

Being a *vegetarian* means that you choose not to eat some or all animal products, like meat, fish, eggs, and dairy. There are lots of ways to be a vegetarian. Some people who call themselves vegetarians don't eat red meat or poultry, but eat fish, eggs, and dairy; others don't eat meat and fish but still eat dairy products; and still others won't eat anything at all that came from an animal (they're called *vegans*). Some people become vegetarians because they want to be healthier. Others do it because they don't want to harm animals or they believe it's better for the environment, or for a combination of all of those reasons.

✓ ***REALITY CHECK*** "I became a vegetarian when I decided that killing animals for food was wrong," says Alex. "When I learned more about it, I found out that there were also health benefits and environmental benefits from a vegetarian diet. The first time I tried being a vegetarian, I soon went back to eating chicken. When I tried it again, I asked my mom to go vegetarian with me to make the transition easier. She agreed, and she's still a vegetarian today. My brother and father still eat meat, though."

❖***LINKS***
If you're interested in learning more about vegetarianism or nutrition in general, check out Appendix A (Learn More) for more books and Web sites to get you going.

If you're interested in going veggie, it's important to make sure you don't just suddenly drop animal products from your meals without adding anything else in, especially if you eat a lot of meat right now. (*Any* major change in what you eat should be done slowly and carefully, and you should talk to your doctor first.) Meat, fish, and dairy supply protein and important vitamins and minerals, like iron, so you'll want to be sure to eat plenty of other foods that provide those nutrients, such as beans and vegetables.

Nutrition everywhere

Now that you know what to eat, how do you make it happen?

☀ ***WORK IT!*** When you're eating at your school cafeteria or at a fast-food place, you don't exactly have an endless gourmet selection. How can you find healthful *and* yummy food wherever you are? Here's how to pick the right stuff . . .

. . . in your cafeteria:

Go ahead and have corn dogs, chicken nuggets, grilled cheese, or whatever your cafeteria does decently. (Even if it's not super nutritious, you've got to eat *something* for energy, right?) But also try these tips:

- Add some kind of vegetable or fruit every day — fruit cup, green beans, applesauce, whatever they're pushing that day.

- Aim to have several different *colors* on your tray. (The more colors you have, the more vitamins you're consuming.) For example, grilled cheese, french fries, and applesauce isn't such a colorful combo. If you can, try adding peas to your plate, having a salad with carrots or tomatoes on it, or grabbing an orange for dessert.

- If you have a choice, pick milk or juice over soda. (Milk is a good source of calcium and vitamin D, which are both needed for growing bones and teeth.)

- If you or your parents don't have time to pack your lunch (or if you don't feel like it!), you can still stick an apple, a box of raisins, or a bag of cherries in your backpack to snack on when there aren't any good choices in the lunch line.

. . . at the food court at the mall:

Fast-food places aren't exactly known for healthful eating, either. But as long as you remember a few little tips, fast food doesn't have to mean *bad food*. (P.S. If you go for an all–junk food meal once in a while, that's okay, as long as you generally eat good stuff the rest of the time.)

- You don't have to give up cheeseburgers and pizza — just try to sneak a vegetable or two in there. Get lettuce, tomato, and mushrooms on your burger, grab some veggie pizza, go for vegetables on the side with your Chinese food instead of an egg roll.

- If you normally chow down on fried foods, sample food that's *not* fried for a change of pace — a baked potato instead of french fries, a grilled chicken sandwich or barbecued chicken pieces instead of crispy, a burrito or soft taco instead of a crunchy taco. Going for *un*fried lets you savor the flavor of the food, not the fried coating.

- When it comes to toppings, think less glop and more crunch. Glop means gooey, gloppy sauces and toppings like mayo, cheese sauce, tartar sauce, and those weird mystery sauces. Crunch means stuff like lettuce, tomato, onions, pickles, and other veggies on sandwiches and nuts on a sundae.

☀"WORK IT!" Eat breakfast every day. By the time you wake up in the morning, you've probably gone ten or more hours without eating, so chow down! Eating breakfast improves your memory, helps you concentrate, makes you more creative, and gives you an important energy boost. If you hate breakfast food, try left-over pizza or pasta — who says breakfast has to be cereal or eggs?

☀"WORK IT!" Go grocery shopping with your parents so you can help pick out tasty, easy, healthful snacks. Some stuff you might want to keep stocked:

baby carrots and other prewashed veggie sticks
cherry tomatoes
boxes of raisins
your favorite fruits, or premade fruit cups
mini yogurt containers or yogurt squeezes
    (they're yummy frozen, too!)
granola bars
string cheese
whole wheat bread or bagels

☀**"WORK IT!"** Team up with your parents and brothers or sisters so feeding your body well and trying new things becomes a family project.

• Use the list of foods at the beginning of this chapter to make your own list of foods and flavors you'd like to try as a family. Make one night a week "New Food Night," when everyone helps cook a meal that has one new food in it (look in cookbooks or online for inspiration). You can take turns deciding what the new food will be.

- Make a chart or calendar where you can track how many fruits and veggies everyone in the family eats every day this week. You can do this really easily by making a grid with seven squares across (for the days of the week) and as many rows as there are people in your family. Label the days of the week, and give each person a row. Decorate the chart with photos or drawings of fruits and veggies, or whatever other kinds of decorations you think of. Use stickers, stars, or check marks to count your servings. Have a contest to see who can eat the most fruits and veggies this week. The winner gets a prize you decide on — maybe control of the remote for a whole week, or having his favorite foods prepared and served by the other family members, or being waited on hand and foot for one day?

✓ ***REALITY CHECK*** No matter what you like to eat, you can squeeze new, more healthful foods into your day pretty painlessly. Check out these food makeovers. (Remember, the info in this chapter should never substitute for a doctor's advice. If you want a *real* food makeover, talk to your doctor, who can give you tips or help you find a registered nutritionist.)

Today **Fiona** ate:

breakfast: granola with skim milk

lunch: veggie sub from Subway, caffeine-free Coke, and lots of strawberries

dinner: a few nachos, a veggie burger, caffeine-free Coke

dessert: frozen yogurt

bedtime: chamomile tea

Since Fiona is a vegetarian, she tends to eat lots of fruits and veggies — yay! She could get even more in by sprinkling berries in her granola or on her frozen yogurt and snacking on veggies or fruits during the day. She could also substitute milk or juice for one of those Cokes. Fiona may not be getting enough protein — adding beans to her nachos, having a yogurt with lunch, tossing some nuts on her frozen yogurt, drinking more milk, or snacking on yogurt or string cheese could help with that.

Today **Caitlin** ate:

breakfast: two eggs, two slices of toast with butter, one percent milk

snack: about five Oreos, water

lunch: ham-and-cheese sandwich on potato bread with Miracle Whip, potato chips, Crystal Light, two Oreos

snack: Rice Krispies Treat, water

dinner: beef stir-fry with peppers and onions, rice, soy sauce, one percent milk

dessert: Rice Krispies Treat, water

Caitlin's an athlete, so she eats lots of food to give her enough energy to get through the day. She drinks lots of water, too, which is great. But she could use way more fruits and vegetables —

right now she has only one or two servings for the day. Subbing real fruit juice for that Crystal Light would be a start, and adding lettuce or tomato to her sandwich, drinking calcium-fortified OJ at breakfast, including an apple at lunch, or eating fruit along with her Rice Krispies Treats would also help. She could also replace those chips with a frozen fruit pop or yogurt (for protein and calcium).

About those snacks — she tends to eat the same things over and over. There's nothing wrong with eating Rice Krispies Treats and Oreos, but replacing one or two of those snacks with berries or veggie sticks would add a little variety *and* add to her fruit and veggie total for the day.

The "D" word

"I've been on a diet for two weeks and all I've lost is two weeks."
— Totie Fields, comedian

You've probably heard people — celebrities, parents, siblings, maybe even your friends — talk about dieting. Maybe you've even thought of trying it. But, in general, dieting is a bad idea, especially when you're still growing. Most kids need

2,000 or more calories a day, which is a lot more food than you probably think it is. Trying to eat less in order to lose weight means you might not get the nutrients you need to grow and won't have enough energy to get through the day. Eating a wide variety of healthful foods and getting active regularly is the best way to keep your body strong and maintain a healthy weight.

✔ ***REALITY CHECK*** "A lot of my friends are on diets because they *think* they are fat," Blair complains. "In reality, they are perfect the way they are and I don't know why they think that they are such cows!"

⚘***LINKS***
See Chapter 3 (Working It) for fun ways to move your bod. Check out Chapter 1 (Discovering Your Body) for more on loving the body you're in.

Hannah says, "I hate dieting. I've seen my mom dieting and I always want to help her eat better instead. Eating should make you feel good, not like you're depriving yourself."

Sydney agrees: "I think diets are pretty pointless, because you're keeping yourself from eating things you need."

There are a lot of people out there who *think* they need to lose weight. But remember, right now your body is constantly changing. **The shape and size you are now is not the way your body is going to be forever.**

It's normal and healthy to gain a lot of weight very quickly while you're in your growth spurt, sometimes before your height catches up. Even though the number on the scale might be more than you're used to, or more than other kids you know weigh, it's probably part of your normal development. Don't compare your body to other kids' bodies, and especially not to grown-up celebrities.

If you're really worried about your weight, talk to your parents and see a doctor, who can help you figure out a healthy way to lose weight — *if* you need to.

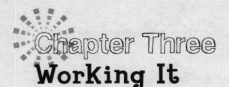

Chapter Three
Working It

Move your bod!

You already know that being active is great for your body — you get stronger, faster, and more flexible, and you have more energy. But it's also great for the *whole* you. Moving your bod regularly helps you sleep better, stress less, think more clearly and creatively, and be in a better mood. Sports and other physical activities also make you feel good about yourself and what your body can do.

✔ ***REALITY CHECK*** Sports are a great outlet for Caitlin. "When I'm on the pitching mound, I can forget about all my problems and just have fun," she says. "I also love the excitement of the games, the rush of adrenaline when you're in a bind and have to work your hardest to get out of it. And it's so much fun to get to know new

✂ ***LINKS***
Flip back to Chapter 1 (Discovering Your Body) to read about appreciating your body for what it can do, not just how it looks. Check out Chapter 4 (Feed Your Brain) for more stuff that keeps you in a great frame of mind.

people on your team, and to work with them so you can win."

"When I dance I'm so happy, moving and flying across the stage," says Fiona. Blair agrees: "Dancing just makes me feel so free. I don't think I could live if I didn't dance."

Even though Natalie doesn't like playing sports, she gets into being active. "After you run a mile or do some sit-ups, you feel really good about yourself," she says.

◄━*WRITE IT!* Which sports or activities are your favorites, and why?

Soccer fun, cool
Roller blading fun exciting
hockey awesome

Which sports or activities are your least favorite, and why?

golf, boring, lame,

_____

_____

"WRITE IT!" Is there a sport or activity you've always wanted to try? What is it?

_____ _Hockey_ _____

Pushing your limits

One cool thing about being active is that you're constantly learning about what your body can do. You've got so much unexplored potential sitting right there in your bod — speeds you haven't reached yet, strength you haven't discovered, flexibility that's waiting to be encouraged. Who knows what your body could do if you tried?

The more you try and the fitter you get, the more you can gradually push yourself to achieve more and more, to become stronger, faster, springier, more flexible, more graceful. And as you keep growing you'll discover endless new things your body is capable of — after all, people your parents' age decide to run marathons! (Pushing your limits _doesn't_ mean ignoring

> **"I do not try to dance better than anyone else. I only try to dance better than myself."**
> **— Mikhail Baryshnikov, dancer**

your body when it's had enough, though. Warm up before any physical activity, stop immediately if you're in pain, and check with a doctor before you take on a major new challenge.)

✔ ***REALITY CHECK*** "Sometimes in gym class we have to swim for twenty minutes, counting how many laps we do," says Christy. "I always set a goal for myself, like forty-five laps, and I raise it a little each time. It's great to see how I'm improving over time."

"I've finally got my left split down," says Fiona, a dancer. "I never even would have considered doing *any* kind of split a few years ago."

"When I was at camp, we all went mountain biking one day," said Natalie. "I never realized how tough it would be, and I didn't think I would be able to finish. But I ended up biking the whole time. I was surprised I made it to the end, and it felt good to know that I had kept up with the guys in front of me."

"My softball team was playing against a team that we had played before and almost beat, and we were really set on beating them," says Caitlin. "They had a pitcher who was very fast and accurate. I was really nervous but I really wanted to win. I matched the other pitcher pitch for pitch, but we still lost the game because of a bad call. But after the game, all the parents and my teammates were telling me how well I pitched against the other team. I was so amazed and proud at how well I pitched under pressure, even though we didn't win."

✹**"WORK IT!"** Nobody's born an Olympic champion, or even a seventh-grade track star. Read a book about a professional athlete's rise to the top to help inspire your own goals. (Ask your teacher or librarian for suggestions, or check out the reading lists at the end of this book.)

✹**"WORK IT!"** Make yourself an inspirational poster or collage. You could include photos of athletes you admire, quotes or sayings that inspire you, a

✂***LINKS***
Flip to the end of this chapter for more on motivating yourself to move your bod.

list of your athletic goals, words that motivate

you (like STRONG or POWER), or anything else
that makes you feel like pushing yourself harder.

Want to see what your body can do? Test your abilities
in a few of these areas:

Strength is important in nearly every sport, from
dancing to wrestling. Every sport uses strength in different ways, and relies on different parts of you to be
strong. Running, jumping rope, or skating requires
strength in your legs, while pitchers need strong arms
and gymnasts need solid but flexible backs and shoulders (among other things!).

☀*"WORK IT!"* Try these activities to explore
your *strength:*

- Jump as high as you can. Try different ways
  to jump higher — curling up more before
  you jump so you get more spring from your
  legs, thrusting your arms up like you're
  grabbing for the ceiling as you jump, making a running leap.
- See how many push-ups, crunches, or pull-
  ups you can do. When doing push-ups, be

sure to keep your body in a straight line — *don't* let your back sag or bubble up. For crunches, lie on your back with your knees bent, feet flat on the floor. Put your hands behind your head and press the back of your head into your hands as you lift your shoulders off the floor. Go slow and concentrate on having your belly muscles do all the work — *don't* pull up on your head and neck. (If you need more help figuring out these moves, ask your gym teacher to show them to you.)

- Have an arm-wrestling contest with a friend.

> **Did you know?**
> During her childhood in the 1940s, athlete Wilma Rudolph contracted polio, which crippled her leg so badly that doctors said she would never walk. Not only did she learn to walk, she became a basketball star in high school and, later, a track star and Olympic champion. At the Rome Olympics in 1960, she became the first American woman to win three gold medals. You can read more about her in *Wilma Unlimited: How Wilma Rudolph Became the World's Fastest Woman,* by Kathleen Krull and illustrated by David Diaz (Voyager Books, 2000).

Flexibility is important in things like tumbling or diving, where you need to be able to fold and stretch your body. But staying flexible is good for you whether you're an athlete or not. Stretching your muscles (especially after you exercise) keeps them from getting stiff and possibly injured.

✹**"WORK IT!"** Try these activities to explore your *flexibility:*

- Stand up, then bend over and try to touch your toes. Keep your legs straight, but don't lock your knees, and *don't* push or force yourself down. How far down can you go? Try doing this every day, holding it for five to ten seconds. (You should feel a slight stretch, but if it hurts, you're going too far.) After a week or so, can you stretch a little farther than you could before?

- Stand on your tiptoes and stretch your hands as high as you can above your head. Try to make your body as long as you can. If you want, grab a pencil and put a tiny mark on the wall as high as you can reach (double-check with your parents first!). See if you can reach higher tomorrow.

- Put your left hand behind your back, reaching up toward your head. With your right hand, try to touch your left hand from above, reaching over your right shoulder. (Again, you should feel a slight stretch, but if it hurts, stop right away!) Switch sides.

- Develop a regular stretching routine that you can do after you exercise or play sports, or before you go to bed. (Ask your gym teacher or coach for help coming up with stretches.) Track your flexibility over a month or so and see if you get bendier as time goes by.

Balance and *coordination* are needed in graceful sports like dancing, but also in any activity where you have to move and turn quickly, like basketball, soccer, ice skating, even hula-hooping.

✴"WORK IT!" Try these activities to explore your *balance* and *coordination*:

- Stand up straight, hands hanging by your sides. Lift your right foot a few inches off the ground. How long can you stand like that? Now try lifting your right leg in front of you as high as you can, knee bent. How long can you stand like that? Try it on your left side. (Have a contest with a friend or sibling to see who can balance the longest!)

- Teach yourself to do a handstand. Practice against a wall or tree first — place your hands on the ground and kick up with your feet — then try it without the wall or tree. If you can already do a handstand, see how long you can walk on your hands without falling.

- Find a long, straight line on the ground — a crack in the sidewalk, a long floorboard in your house, the border between your lawn and your driveway. Pretend that line is a tightrope and try to walk along it without falling off. When you can walk the "tight-rope" easily, try hopping on one foot, twirling, or leaping along it.

Endurance is especially important in activities like distance running or swimming, where you have to go a long time without stopping. Even running to catch the bus or having a marathon shopping day requires endurance!

WORK IT! Try these activities to explore your *endurance:*

- Do jumping jacks at a moderate speed — not superfast, not superslow. Count how many you can do before you poop out. (If anything starts to hurt or you're gasping for air, stop right away.)
- Time yourself to see how long you can jog, bike, skate, or swim without stopping. Can you try to go one minute longer tomorrow?

WORK IT! Design an obstacle course for you and your friends that challenges your strength, endurance, flexibility, and coordination. For example, you could have participants do a limbo, leap over a tree stump, run while weaving back and forth between cans or stones, jog in place for twenty seconds, jump up and grab a tree branch, and finally hop on

✂️*LINKS*
To find more
new ways to
explore what
your body can
do, check out
some of the
fitness books in
Appendix A
(Learn More).

one foot across the finish line. Get creative with it — use every corner of your yard or park!

Making it happen

To keep your body at its best, it's ideal to get moving *regularly*. Aim to get active every day for at least fifteen to thirty minutes — that means doing something that makes your heart beat faster, your breathing quicken, and your skin break a sweat. (You'll find tons of suggestions in the **☀️*WORK IT!***s on pages 87–94.)

You don't have to join a team or have an exercise plan to get moving. Maybe team sports aren't your style, or you don't have time to join a club, or you'd just rather crash in front of the TV or computer. (Believe me, I can relate.) You can keep fit and active by doing fun things right at home, too. Some important things to keep in mind:

1. **Have fun.** When you're playing games or running around with friends, the last thing you're thinking about is "exercise." So try to find activities that are fun for you. Try different sports

until you find one you like. Mix it up so you're always doing different stuff (blading, playing touch football with your friends, teaching yourself gymnastic stunts, setting up relay race tournaments with the neighborhood kids, having snowball fights) — that way you won't get bored. Designate the hour after you get home from school as "playtime," and use it.

> **"The first thing is to love your sport. Never do it to please someone else. It has to be yours."**
> **— Peggy Fleming, former U.S., World, and Olympic figure skating champion**

✓ **"REALITY CHECK"** "I hate exercise," says Mallory. "But I find things I like to do, like sports. Being involved in a game takes the work out of it and makes it fun. When I'm not doing sports, I like to buy videos, like dance or Tae Bo, where I can just learn cool moves and have fun."

Hannah likes to keep things fun, too. "My favorite exercise is swimming," she says. "When I was really little, I always loved to swim. Everyone called me a fish because I was constantly in the water. My parents got me to sign up for a team, and I love it — I made a ton of new friends. I also love going for walks. I take walks with a friend of mine all the time, and we just walk around the neighborhood and talk for hours. *And* I just took a kickboxing class. My normal routine was getting boring, so I mixed it up a little and discovered something I now love!"

"I started playing soccer when I was six, because my mom saw that I had a lot of extra energy," says Gretchen. "I just found my diary from when I was little, and it was all about my first soccer practice and how much I loved it!"

2. **Everyone's good at something.** When I was in middle school, I took tons of tennis lessons, year after year. But my gangly, overgrown arms and legs kept tripping me up — I was growing so quickly, I was pretty uncoordinated, and I could never quite get the hang of hitting that ball. I hated it. However, when I decided to try the swim team, it turned out that my long reach was perfect for slipping through the water. I discovered that in the water, I could actually be graceful.

   If you're lucky, you already know what you're good at. But maybe you've found that no matter how hard you try, the sport you're doing just isn't working for you. It's okay to keep trying different things until you find something that clicks. **The more things you try, the more you'll learn about your body and what it can do.** So try everything: baseball, soccer, swimming, tennis, dancing, skateboarding, rock climbing, running, martial arts, whatever you can! (See the ✳️***WORK IT!*** sections for more ideas.)

✔️ ***REALITY CHECK*** Sometimes you find something you love almost by accident, the way Christy found color guard. "I just heard an announcement about it in middle school," she explains. "I'd seen the flags in parades and thought it looked fun, so I tried out. None of my friends did it — I just did it for myself because it looked like something I could do. I ended up enjoying it a lot. It works your upper body strength and is just as physical as any other sport. It's a physical and mental challenge."

Alex got into skateboarding randomly, too. "My uncle bought me a cheap board when I

was in fourth grade, and I slowly progressed —
really, really slowly!"

"When I was in third grade, a dance studio
opened up down the street from me," says
Jolene. "I lived in a really small town and there
wasn't much to do, and I thought dancing
would be a good way to entertain myself. My
mom and I went and checked it out and I
signed up for tap and jazz."

Just because you don't like one kind of
sport or exercise doesn't mean you won't like
others. "I hate running laps in gym class — I get
so exhausted," says Caitlin. "But I love it when
we play team sports, because that's fun."

"I don't like running, but horseback riding is
great," says Natalie. "I didn't think skiing was
very cool, so I tried snowboarding because I
wanted to look cooler. It's actually really fun!"

3. **Don't overdo it.** It's great to push yourself to do
   better, but getting injured is no fun. Some
   people even make themselves sick by exercising
   too much. **Always listen to your body** and pay
   attention when it's sending you signals that

something is wrong. If something you're doing hurts, or if you feel sick or dizzy, stop right away.

Start any activity with light warm-ups, so your body can gradually work up to more effort. (When your muscles are all warmed up, you're less likely to get injured.) For example, you could walk for five minutes before you start sprinting, do some easy jumping jacks and stretches before you strap on your skis, or jog around the soccer field before a game. Drink water before, during, and after you exercise. And if you never do anything active now, take it slowly — check with a doctor before you start anything new, and build up your level of activity gradually.

"WORK IT!" Try some of these sports or activities on for size. (By the way, this is obviously not a list of every sport in the world, so don't get mad if I left your favorite out!) Many of these you can try in a structured setting, like joining a school team or local club league, but if you don't like teams, you can also have fun with them on your own or with friends. For

some of these, you may want to take lessons when you're first getting into it — ask your parents or gym teacher to help you find out where you can get started. Remember, you don't have to be perfect or even good at something to enjoy it. The important thing is that you're learning and having fun, not that you're the best.

badminton

baseball/softball

basketball

bowling

cheerleading

cycling

dancing (ballet, jazz, tap, hip-hop, ballroom, Latin, dance team, or even dancing around your room)

football

gymnastics

hiking

hockey (ice hockey, field hockey, roller hockey)

lacrosse

martial arts (tae kwon do, judo, and karate are just a few of the traditional martial arts

you can try. For a modern twist, try a kickboxing or Tae Bo video.)

miniature golf

Ping-Pong

rock climbing (Many gyms, rec centers, and
even malls have rock-climbing walls where
you can try it out and get a lesson.)

rowing

skateboarding

skating (ice skating, in-line skating, even old-
fashioned roller skating)

skiing (cross-country, downhill, or water)

snowboarding

soccer

surfing (body or board)

swimming

tennis

track

volleyball

wrestling

yoga (Try an easy beginner's video, or check
out a class at the local Y or health club.)

✴ *WORK IT!* Who says getting active has to be about sports? These activities are so much fun, the word *exercise* won't even cross your mind:

- Walk the dog, then take an extra jog around the block just for kicks (the pooch will love it).
- Race someone to the end of the street or around your yard.
- Get out a jump rope and see how many times you can jump in a minute (have someone time you). Or make up a jump-roping rhyme about your school, or one that uses each of your friends' names, and skip it out.
- Build the most massive, elaborate snow fort ever, or create a family of snow giants.
- Invent a silly race — like one in which you have to slap the ground every three steps, or one in which you have to flap your arms and scream at the top of your lungs as you run, or one in which you have to swim while pressing your elbows to your sides and blowing bubbles.
- Run through the sprinkler. Don't forget to try

running backward, doing cartwheels, and other tricks.

- Rake up a huge pile of leaves, then run and dive into it.

- Have a dorky dance contest: Pick a fast-paced dance song, then compete with your friends to see who can come up with the silliest, most spastic dance moves ever.

- Organize a neighborhood-wide game of tag, hide-and-seek, or tug-of-war.

- Fly a kite — be sure to run with it.

- See how far you can swim underwater.

- Make up your own water aerobics or syn-chronized swimming routines (best when done with friends!).

- Find the biggest, snowiest hill you can and sled down it.

- Design a new sport to play with your friends. It could be a variation on a sport you already play (like basketball using a beach ball), a kind of theme tag (like Harry Potter tag or *Star Wars* tag), a combination of two or more sports (like a Ping-Pong relay race), or something totally unique.

Even if you're really busy, you can fit little bits of activity into your everyday life.

✂ *LINKS*
See *Spirit*,
Chapter 2
(What Matters
to You — and
Why It Matters),
for more on
making room in
your life for the
things that are
important to
you.

✔ ***REALITY CHECK*** "There are always activities that you can do with friends that are good exercise, like shopping, dancing, or bowling," says Hannah. "Sometimes I do toning exercises while I'm watching TV or baby-sitting. And I always take the stairs instead of the elevator!"

"I actually study while I exercise," says Christy. "One night I had two tests the next day and I was extremely stressed. I took my notes down to the basement where we have exercise equipment and rode the stationary bike while I studied my notes. I was getting in exercise and studying at the same time! Plus, it made me less stressed!"

☀ ***WORK IT!*** Squeeze in these sneaky sweat-working moves whenever you get a chance:

- Take the stairs or walk up the escalator at the mall (bonus if you take the steps two at a time).

- Walk, bike, or skate to school, practice, or a friend's house, instead of getting a ride.

- Let the ice-cream truck pass your house, then sprint down the sidewalk to catch up to it.

- Put the phone across the room so you have to get up and run to answer it.

- Every time you finish a problem in your math homework, do sit-ups, push-ups, or jumping jacks corresponding to the answer — so if the answer to the problem is 42, do 42 jumping jacks. If the answer is $2/3$, do two sit-ups and three push-ups.

- Volunteer to carry all the groceries into the house.

- Do jumping jacks, jump rope, or jog in place during commercial breaks of your favorite TV show. That can add up to as much as fifteen minutes of jumping jacks during an hour-long show!

- Dance along when you're watching music videos or listening to the radio.

- Forced to help clean the bathroom or kitchen? Have your mom or dad spray cleaner all over the floor. Tie rags to your feet, and boogie all over the room until the floor's clean.

Keeping it up

So you want to get active every day, but you're not sure how to keep it going after a week or two. Even the sportiest kids need help motivating once in a while. When you feel bored, mix it up. You can introduce a variation on something you already do, like finding a new running path or teaching yourself to skate backward, or try something completely different, like diving into swimming if you're a baseball player or trying rock climbing instead of gymnastics.

You can also try one of these ideas for giving yourself a kick start:

✳*WORK IT!* Get an "active buddy" — a friend who will go in-line skating with you, play catch, or do whatever other sporty stuff you can dream up. It's a lot easier — and more fun! — to stick to being active every day if someone else is doing it with you.

☀*WORK IT!* Turn family bonding time into a sweat session. Instead of having a family game night, why not go hiking or bike riding together? Or make a once-a-week date to go jogging or play tennis with your mom or dad — they'll *love* having the special time with you, and you'll both get off your butts. You could also schedule an annual Thanksgiving family football game, or a Fourth of July swim meet. (As you know, once something becomes a family tradition, it's impossible to get out of!)

☀*WORK IT!* Trade daily "adventure assignments" with a friend. At the end of the school day, each of you gives the other a slip of paper (or sends the other an e-mail) with an activity to complete at home or together — like "Do twenty cartwheels," "Walk to the library and back," or "Dance to these five songs." (You can also assign each other healthful snacks to try or creative activities to sample.) If you want to do this with a group of friends, put all your slips in an envelope and draw them at random.

WORK IT! Make a move-it plan. Try one of these ideas:

Write it out. Grab a calendar and outline a monthlong program for yourself. Pick one activity from this chapter for each day of the month. Write them down on the calendar so you remember what you've got planned. (You can change your mind that day if you're in the mood for something different — the point is to plan something active for each day.) Mix it up according to your schedule — if soccer practice is every Tuesday and Thursday, that's your activity for those days. If Friday is your big TV night, jot down "jumping jacks during commercial breaks" as Friday's activity. Plan longer or tougher stuff for weekends, when you'll have more time. When you complete a day's activity, check off that day on your calendar or put a big sticker on it.

Color-code it. Divide up a list of activities into different categories. You could do it by difficulty (hard/medium/easy), style (inside/outside or group/solo), or use the categories that the ☀**"WORK IT!"** sections on pages 87–94 are in: sports/fun/sneaky. Assign each category a color, then grab a calendar and color each day a different shade. Write out the lists of activities and post them next to your colored calendar. Every day, pick an activity that corresponds to that day's color, and do it.

Make mini-goals. Want a plan that's a little more focused, less random? Set yourself small, reasonable, specific goals, one at a time. That means things like "I want to be able to do ten push-ups" or "I want to run for five minutes without pooping out," not "I want to get super-buff" or "I want to run a marathon." Every time you make a goal, give yourself a little reward, like funky new shoelaces or a new CD. Then set a new goal!

Chapter Four
Feed Your Brain

Stretching your mind

Would you believe me if I told you that you're smarter than all the adults you know? Here's why: Right around now, your brain is going through a huge surge in development, kind of like the growth spurt your body goes through. Because of all the brain growth that happens at your age, your brain is really flexible and great at adding new information — so you're much better than adults at picking up languages, mastering new concepts, and other types of learning.

Since you're so smart, it's fun to explore what your brain can do and stretch it as far as you can. Just like it's important to keep your body moving and flexing, it's good to work your mind, too, to keep it in top shape. Take advantage of your supercharged brain and try these brain benders and exercises:

✳ *LINKS*
Turn to
Creativity,
Chapter 5
(Curiosity
Counts), for
more on
stretching your
brain by feeding
your curiosity.

✳ *WORK IT!* Out loud or in your head, count backward from 100 by fives: 100, 95, 90, 85 . . . Now count backward by sevens: 100, 93, 86, 79 . . . How quickly can you do it?

✳*WORK IT!* Pick a poem to memorize. (Ask a teacher or librarian to recom- mend books of poetry that you can look through.) Try to pick one that's at least twenty lines long. Memorize it two or three lines at a time: Start with the first two lines, then add two more each day, until you can recite the whole thing.

> **✂*LINKS***
> **Check out** *Creativity*, **Chapter 3 (Write On), for more on poetry and the power of writing.**

✳*WORK IT!* Play Pictionary or charades, with a twist (pick one):

- All the answers have to start with the letter "A" (or another letter of your choice).
- Pictionary: Draw everything upside down.
- Charades: Act out the clues without using your hands.

▶*WRITE IT!* Write a tongue twister. (Hint: A good tongue twister usually repeats the

same or similar sounds in different combinations. "She sells seashells by the seashore" repeats "s" and "sh" and "ee" and "ell" again and
again.) Challenge your parents, friends, or sibs
to say it!

_____

_____

_____

✴️*WORK IT!* Get together with a friend and
a stack of your favorite CDs. Have your friend
play the first three seconds of a song and see if
you can guess what it is.

✴️*WORK IT!* Suppose your allowance is set
up so that every week you get twice as much
money as you got the week before. Week one
you get $1, week two $2, week three $4, week
four $8, and so on. Every week you put the
money into the bank. How many weeks would
it be before you had more than $100 total?
Before you had more than $1,000 total? (*See
the end of this chapter for the answer!)

※"WORK IT!" On a piece of paper, draw a shape that you could cut out in one piece and fold into a cube.

"WRITE IT!" A *palindrome* is a word or phrase that is the same forward and backward, like "noon," "Madam, I'm Adam," "radar." How many palindromes can you think of?

_____   _____

_____   _____

_____   _____

_____   _____

"WRITE IT!" An *anagram* is when you re-arrange the letters of a word or phrase to create a new word or phrase. How many anagrams can you make of your name or a friend's name? (For example, my name, Jeannie Kim, can be rearranged to make the phrase "I jam in knee" or the name "Jamie N. Nike.") Throw in your middle name, too, if you want more letters to work with!

_____   _____

_____   _____

_____   _____

_____   _____

LINKS
Check out
Appendix A
(Learn More)
for more places
to find cool
brain benders.

WORK IT! Design a brainteasing scavenger hunt. For example, you could include things like "an object whose name is a palindrome," "something you eat that's brown," "a toy that was invented before 1980" — anything that people have to think about before they can hunt for it.

Which smart are you?

You'll notice that not every brain exercise in the previous section involved math problems or logic games. That's because there are many different kinds of smarts. Not all of them are taught in school, but they are all important.

Everyone is naturally gifted in one or more areas of smarts, like visual smarts, musical smarts, numbers and logic smarts, body smarts, word smarts, or social smarts. And no matter what kind of smarts you already have, you can always explore and develop your smarts in other areas.

✓ *REALITY CHECK* "School subject-wise, I'm good at math and science," says Christy. "But I'm also known for being a very creative person as well. I love singing and I love art. I like that there is no such thing as being perfect in the arts."

"I'm good at social skills," says Alaina. "Even though I'm shy, I'm still a good listener and talker. I help people out when they have problems and I listen when they need to vent."

"I feel smartest when I prove a point or win a fight," says Sarah. "Even though it's not school related, it makes me feel more intelligent, because I don't think book smarts are everything."

"My big thing is music," says Alex. "I have a really good ear and I can usually figure songs out by listening to them. And my dad was a math teacher, so I have to be good at that!"

 **QUIZ: What kind of smart are you?**

Take this quiz to explore your natural abilities and discover how to develop other brain areas, too!

Check off all the statements that are true for you:

1. I'm good at remembering songs, lyrics, and melodies — sometimes after hearing them just once.
2. Whenever there's a fight in my group of friends, I'm likely to be the one to smooth things out.
3. I have a really good vocabulary.
4. Gym is one of my favorite classes!
5. I'm always humming to myself or tapping out rhythms with my hands and feet.
6. It's important to me that my room looks just right — I spend lots of time arranging things, putting up new posters, or picking out the perfect color bedspread or rug.
7. I rock at charades.

8. Math and science classes are usually my favorites.

9. I can generally tell when people around me are upset or unhappy.

10. If a movie has bad music, it ruins it for me.

11. I love taking pictures to remember important events.

12. People are always coming to me for advice when they have problems.

13. I'm really curious about how things work and am always trying to find logical explanations for things.

14. I enjoy writing stories and poems.

15. When I see a movie, I always notice little details about the costumes, lighting, and scenery.

16. I like making lists and planning my time efficiently.

17. If I've heard a song enough times, I can usually pick it out on the piano or another instrument.

18. When I talk, I tend to gesture and move around a lot to illustrate what I'm saying.

19. I'm good at organizing people to do stuff, like getting a group together for a party or persuading everyone to go to a movie I want to see.
20. I can talk my way out of anything.
21. I have a pretty good sense of direction.
22. I like working with my hands and doing crafty projects, like building models, sewing, or woodworking.
23. I'm good at telling jokes and saying funny things.
24. It drives me crazy when someone sings off-key.
25. I can add up numbers in my head pretty quickly.
26. Picking up new dance moves is easy for me.
27. I couldn't live without my diary.
28. I'm constantly drawing or doodling things.
29. My room is totally organized, with every-thing in its proper place.
30. I make friends easily.

Each statement corresponds to a different type of intelligence. The category or categories where you checked off the *most* statements are the ones in which you're the strongest. Read on to find out how to make your smarts work for you — and be sure to read the other categories to find out how you can build up other kinds of smarts as well!

Musical smarts (numbers 1, 5, 10, 17, 24)

You're sensitive to music, rhythm, and sounds of all kinds — you're the first one to hear when the bathroom faucet is dripping! Chances are you have a nice singing voice and a good memory for melody and rhythm. You love being surrounded by music, whether it's on your CD player or computer or bopping away in your own head, and you *always* have an opinion about what you're listening to. **Work it by . . .** picking up an instrument (if you don't play one already), joining a choir, or starting your own. **Use it in school by . . .** making up musical jingles to help you memorize stuff.

LINKS
Check out *Creativity*, Chapter 2 (Performing the Arts), for more on exploring your musical side.

Social smarts (numbers 2, 9, 12, 19, 30)

You rock at relating to other people and understanding where they're coming from. Because you're so good at getting along, you're a natural leader or organizer, as well as an awesome friend. Other people turn to you because of your extra-sharp empathy, and you know just what to say to make them feel better. The sneaky side: Your ability to figure other people out also makes you good at getting them to do what *you* want! **Work it by . . .** becoming a peer counselor or running for student government. **Use it in school by . . .** organizing study groups or doing homework with a friend.

> ❋❋***LINKS***
> ***Friends and Family* has tons more on getting along with the people in your life.**

Word smarts (numbers 3, 14, 20, 23, 27)

Shakespeare, anyone? Okay, maybe you're not writing five-act plays, but you do have a gift for putting words together, whether in a short story, an editorial for the school paper, a speech in class, or a hilariously sarcastic comment. You're great at ex-

> ❋❋***LINKS***
> **Turn to *Creativity*, Chapter 3 (Write On), to explore your wordy ways even more.**

pressing yourself, so arguing and explaining things come naturally. You love reading and writing, and you probably keep a journal or write awesome letters to your friends. **Work it by . . .** writing for the school paper or literary magazine, composing witty e-mails to your friends, or joining the debate team. **Use it in school by . . .** writing kick-butt reports, taking the best notes, and speaking up in class.

Body smarts (numbers 4, 7, 18, 22, 26)

You've got a gift for moving your body. You probably have excellent coordination and balance, and you enjoy sports and other physical activities. Movement isn't just about exercise for you, though — you use it to express yourself to the world, whether it's through a complicated dance move, a swordfight onstage, or a simple hand gesture. Sitting around pondering is not your style — you like hands-on activities and are a whiz at anything crafty. **Work it by . . .** play-

> ✂ ***LINKS***
> **Chapter 3 (Working It) is full of ways to use your talent for sports and keep that smart bod of yours moving. *Creativity*, Chapter 2 (Performing the Arts) has more on using your knack for expressive movement in theater and dance.**

ing sports or joining the drama club or an improv group. **Use it in school by . . .** crafting kick-butt dioramas and other hands-on projects; taking lots of breaks while you study or do homework to jog, dance around, or do something else physical while your brain absorbs the info.

Visual smarts (numbers 6, 11, 15, 21, 28)

Picture this: You've got a knack for absorbing everything you see. While your super-vision means you're probably great at drawing, painting, sculpture, and other visual arts, you also have a sense of color, space, and environment that's helpful in design, decoration, and finding your way around strange places. You remember things best when you see them, so you prefer maps to verbal directions, videos to radio, and films to lectures. **Work it by . . .** taking an art or design class, making your own movies, or redecorating your room. **Use it in school by . . .** mak-

∗LINKS∗
Dive into all kinds of visual fun and games in *Creativity,* **Chapter 1 (Discover Your Inner Artist).**

ing charts, diagrams, and pictures to help you remember things.

Math/logic smarts (numbers 8, 13, 16, 25, 29)

Your brain is great at anything logical or numbers-based. You're a natural problem solver and experimenter, which makes you especially skilled at methodical subjects like science, math, and computers. Your experimental bent is fed by your natural curiosity, which drives you to find out how things work and why the world is the way it is. Along with word smarts, this is the kind of smarts that schools typically emphasize the most, and you're probably an organized, well-prepared student. **Work it by . . .** building your own Web site, coming up with award-winning science-fair experiments, or investing your allowance. **Use it in school by . . .** organizing a homework schedule for yourself and applying your investigative skills in writing detailed reports.

❖***LINKS***
Feed your curiosity in *Creativity,* **Chapter 5 (Curiosity Counts).**

The care and feeding of your brain

Of course, all that brilliance doesn't just come from nowhere. There's lots that you can do to keep your brain in top shape. Exercise is one thing that helps your brain work better. Another thing you can do is to make sure you're eating plenty of the right foods to keep your brain powering along.

Check out these **foods that keep you smart**. They're all part of a healthful eating style, and are especially good to munch on while you're studying.

Protein, especially *fish*, gives you energy and helps boost brainpower.

> study snack: tuna fish sandwich, apple smeared with peanut butter

Avocado helps you focus and improves memory.

> study snack: veggies dipped in guacamole

Eggs and *milk* contain a substance called choline, which some people say improves brainpower.

> study snack: scrambled eggs or egg salad, a glass of milk, chocolate pudding

✂ ***LINKS***
Turn to Chapter 2 (Eat Up!) for more on foods to keep you functioning.

Fruits and *vegetables* keep brain cells in top

working order. *Blueberries* and other colorful fruits are especially good — they've been shown to help memory and balance.

> study snack: fruit salad, vegetable sticks, cereal with blueberries

Water keeps your energy level up and helps you stay focused. Your brain is mostly water, so it makes sense that when you don't drink enough, it's harder to think straight.

> study snack: a big glass of water or 100 percent fruit juice

Avoid: super-sugary treats and drinks. They'll give you a temporary energy boost, but then you'll crash just as fast — not what you need when you're cramming for a big test!

✓ ***REALITY CHECK*** "My favorite study snacks are definitely apples and carrots. They help me think!" says Mallory.

Getting enough *sleep* is also important for your brain. While you're sleeping, your brain reorganizes and refreshes itself, so if you don't get enough sleep, your brain can't work at its best.

You need at least eight hours of sleep each night, and as you head into your teens, you'll need even more. Unfortunately, between staying up late watching TV or doing homework and dragging out of bed early to go to school, it's hard to get anywhere near that much sleep. It doesn't help that by the time you're ten or eleven, your body just naturally starts to want to go to sleep later and later — and most schools don't seem to want to cooperate by making school start at ten A.M.!

✔ ***REALITY CHECK*** "I usually get between four and six hours of sleep a night," says Heidi. "I don't think it's enough, but my body won't fall asleep until at least twelve, even if I lie down at, say, ten. I'm tired a lot, and I always have trouble getting up in the morning. My mind wanders a lot in class, too."

Without enough sleep, you get cranky, fall asleep in class or on the bus, can't concentrate, and have trouble making decisions and thinking rationally. Lack of sleep can even make it harder for your body to fight off infections and repair itself when you're injured.

✎⃝→°WRITE IT!° **QUIZ: Are you snoozing smart?**

Find out if your sleep habits are helping you or holding you back.

1. Your alarm clock is:
    a. barely needed. You usually pop right out of bed in the morning feeling well rested and ready to go.
    b. a necessary evil. When it goes off, you groan and burrow into your pillow, but eventually drag yourself out of bed.
    c. your worst enemy. You dread hearing it in the morning and you always hit the snooze button a half dozen times before you force your eyes open.
2. On weekends, you like to:
    a. go to bed and get up more or less at the same time you do during the week.
    b. stay up a little later and sleep in a couple hours later than usual.
    c. spend half the day sleeping — you're always exhausted.

3. How often do you drift off during the day?

   a. Hardly ever.

   b. Once in a while, like during a long bus or car ride, or when there's a *really* boring film in class.

   c. All the time — sitting in class, watching TV, doing homework, the ten-minute drive to the grocery store . . .

4. Right before bed, you're likely to be:

   a. relaxing and winding down, maybe listening to quiet music or taking a bath.

   b. watching TV, talking on the phone, or messing around on the computer.

   c. cramming in last-minute homework or freaking out about all the stuff you have to do tomorrow.

5. Do you have trouble focusing during the first couple hours at school?

   a. No — not more than any other time of day!

   b. Sometimes, like if you were up extra late the night before or if class is really boring.

   c. All the time — you don't really get going until around lunchtime.

Mostly a's: Nice work — you're getting plenty of sleep and have great snooze-friendly habits. To keep your brain in top rested condition, don't skimp on sleep when you need it most — when you've got tons of homework or life's a little hectic. Stay sleep smart and keep up your regular routine so you'll always have enough brain juice to get through the day.

Mostly b's: You're probably a little sleep deprived, but it's nothing an extra hour or two here and there can't fix. In addition to going to bed a little earlier on school nights, try going to bed and getting up at close to the same time on the weekends as you do during the week — that way you won't have trouble falling asleep on Sunday nights. To maximize your sleep quality, get your z's in total darkness — no night-lights or flickering TV screen — and throw open your shades to greet the sun as soon as you wake up. (The light signals to your brain that sleep time is over.)

Mostly c's: Yikes! You're running dangerously low on your snooze quota. You're stumbling through your day on way less than total brain capacity, which is why you tend to drift off and have trouble concentrating. Start going to bed fifteen minutes earlier than usual, then keep moving your bedtime earlier until you're able to get up without too much struggle. (You may need to sleep ten or eleven hours a night for a while to help make up your sleep debt!) If you have trouble falling asleep, develop a relaxing bedtime routine to help you wind down — take a bath, drink milk or herbal tea, listen to mellow music, and don't do anything stressful or watch loud TV before bed.

P.S. If you're still dragging through the day after you improve your sleep habits, talk to your parents and check with a doctor. Low energy, extreme sleepiness, insomnia (trouble falling asleep), and difficulty concentrating can also be caused by depression and some health problems.

The big brain buster

When you're worrying about one thing, it's hard to concentrate on something else. For example, when you fight with a friend, you might have a hard time focusing on your homework, or if you're having problems at school, you might feel distracted during soccer practice.

Feeling tense, worried, or overwhelmed can be a major brain drain. When your worries start interfering with you being your best, that's called *stress*. As you get older, you may sometimes find yourself getting stressed out. While it's normal to feel anxious, worried, or even stressed once in a while, there's a lot you can do to help keep stress out of your life.

Everyone has different things that get them wound up, whether it's problems with friends, tons of school-work, or family getting on your case. Even exploring the whole you can be a little overwhelming, if you try to do too many new things at once.

✔ ***REALITY CHECK*** "My best friend stresses me out," says Jenie. "Most of the time we have fun, but sometimes she gets really moody and annoying." Friends are stressful for Jolene, too: "I moved in the middle of seventh grade and it was hard to make new friends. I hated being the new girl!"

"I hate it when I have lots of things to do in a really short time," says Tasha. "For example, some nights I have play practice until 6 P.M., then I come home and have to cram in my homework and taking a shower."

"I get stressed out when plans I had get messed up, or when I'm having a bad day," says Sydney.

Just because life is getting a little crazy doesn't mean your brain has to go with it. When you're feeling wound-up or worried about something, try some of these ideas to help you relax and give your brain a boost:

✴*WORK IT!* Breathe. Stand up straight, your legs about hip-width apart, shoulders back, your arms hanging loosely at your sides. Pretend that there's an invisible string running from the top of your head to the ceiling, pulling your spine straight. Close your eyes and breathe deeply, in and out, through your nose. Imagine that your bad feelings are melting off your body and dripping onto the floor.

✴*WORK IT!* Eat an apple. But don't just eat it, really focus all of your senses on the experience. Inhale the scent (the smell of green apples is calming), savor the crunch as you bite into it, taste the tartness on your tongue. Diving into something with all your senses helps take you out of whatever is worrying you.

✺*WORK IT!* Light a candle. (Check with your parents before you get out the matches!) Try a soothing smell like lavender or vanilla.

✺*WORK IT!* Take a walk, dance around your room, or do something else physical. Moving your body helps release tension and clears your mind.

✂*LINKS*
Flip to Chapter 3 (Working It) for more on the benefits of getting moving.

✺*WORK IT!* Imagine that your tension and worries are a big black blob sitting on top of your head. Close your eyes and concentrate on pouring all the yucky stuff out of your brain and into the blob. Reach up, grab the blob, scrunch it into a ball, and throw it out the window as hard as you can.

✂ *LINKS*
Check out
Friends and
Family **for more**
on how the
folks in your life
can help you
relax — and
how you can
help them, too.

✹ *WORK IT!* Rub it out. Get a friend or your mom or dad to give you a back or neck rub. Be sure to return the favor!

✹ *WORK IT!* Stretch it out. Wherever you are, inhale deeply and stretch your arms up above your head as high as you can reach. (You can do this sitting down, but it's even better if you stand up and get your whole body into the stretch.) You should feel like your spine is getting longer and your rib cage is expanding. Release the stretch slowly as you exhale. If you want, shake your arms and legs around to get out every last little bit of twitchiness.

✹ *WORK IT!* Laugh your butt off. Belly laughing is an all-natural way to loosen up. Keep handy a tape of your favorite silly movie or TV show, or read a funny book or magazine.

☀*WORK IT!* Head outside. Jump in a pile of leaves, run around the block, or just stare at a pond or creek or tree. Breathing fresh air and enjoying nature can help clear your head.

✒*WRITE IT!* Write it out. When you write about what's bothering you, it helps you spew out stress and leave it behind.

> **⚛*LINKS***
> Check out *Creativity* for cool journal ideas and other creative inspirations.

☀*WORK IT!* Create something. Painting, sewing, cooking, making music, or doing anything creative helps you relax and distracts you from whatever's making you jittery.

✔*REALITY CHECK* "When I'm stressed, I usually take a long, hot shower," says Alex. "Listening to music or creating music also helps a lot, especially playing drums."

Jolene relaxes by dancing, singing in the shower, or shopping. Sydney says that when she's freaking out about something, "I talk to my friend Jil, who has helped me out of every slip I've had this year, and I love her for it."

Jody says, "Sometimes I just sit up in my room and write about the things going on that are stressing me out. That usually makes me feel less stressed, and then I can either move on or try to fix the problems that are making me stressed."

"I exercise when I have a hard test the next day," says Christy. "Only for about ten minutes — I usually run one mile. When I'm really stressed, I run like the wind, because it helps me let out aggression and takes my mind off the test."

Of course, the best way to relax is to avoid getting tense in the first place! For some people, that's easy. They're easygoing and don't get too worked up when life gets tough or annoying. If you're one of those people, keep it up! Personally, I'm not that lucky. All my life, I've been the kind of person who gets tense and freaked out very, *very* easily. (If you asked any of my friends, they would definitely agree!) Fight with a friend? I'd torture myself for hours, wondering what

> ✂ *LINKS*
> You can read more about finding peace in *Spirit,* Chapter 6 (Peace Out!).

I could have said differently. Huge assignment due the next day? I'd lock myself in my room, slaving over it and snapping at anyone who dared disturb me, and lie awake half the night worrying if I did an okay job. Sometimes I'd spend more time freaking out about the assignment than actually doing it!

So if you're not naturally easygoing, how do you keep stress from happening? Here are some things that have worked for me. I'm not perfect — I still worry a lot and freak out about things — but this stuff helps keep it to a minimum.

1. **Take good care of yourself.** When you have a lot to do, it's easy to skimp on sleep and pack in the junk food. But the better you take care of your body and brain (by eating well, getting active regularly, sleeping enough, and having people in your life who care about you and support you), the less likely you are to go crazy when things get tough.

2. **Figure out your own signs of stress.** When I'm under pressure, I fidget and jiggle my legs a lot. Sometimes I get really distracted and clumsy because I'm worrying about whatever's making

me tense. Other times I just want to plop down on the couch and eat ice cream. I also tend to snap at whoever is unlucky enough to get in my way!

What are the warning signs that *you're* getting tense? Everyone's signs are different. Some examples might be: getting headaches or stomachaches, having cravings for chocolate, being nasty and sarcastic to people. When you learn to recognize your stress signals, you can immediately take time out when you see them and do something to help yourself relax.

✂❖*LINKS*
See Chapter 2 (Eat Up!) and Chapter 3 (Working It) for more on taking care of your body. *Friends and Family* is all about building great friendships and relationships with the people around you.

◀▪*WRITE IT!* What are some of your personal freak-out signs? (If you're not sure, try asking your parents — they might be able to spot signs of tension in you before you notice them yourself!)

_____

_____

_____

✹*WORK IT!* Using paint, crayon, clay, collage, pizza faces, or whatever artistic medium you like best, create an image that represents the way you feel when you're worried or tense. Then make one that shows you feeling peaceful.

✹*WORK IT!* Sometimes other people aren't so good at noticing your stress signs. Invent a code word or other way to signal your friends and family when you're feeling tense and need some alone time (or hugs!). Next time you feel your stress level rising, blurt out your code word ("Banana!") or do your agreed-on signal (like tying a red ribbon on your bedroom doorknob) so everyone knows not to bug you.

3. **Learn what stresses you out.** If you can figure out the kinds of situations that aggravate you, you can figure out how to avoid or manage those situations. So, if you discover that not having enough time to do your homework makes you crazy, you could work out a plan to manage your time so you're not always leaving

it to the last minute. If performing in a play or concert ties you up in knots, you could find some relaxation exercises to do right before you go onstage (plus rehearse well to make yourself feel more confident). If problems with friends keep you up at night, maybe you could start a journal or make a habit of talking to your parents about what's bothering you.

☀ *WORK IT!* Keep a "stress log." For the next two to four weeks, write down anything that makes you feel worried or tense. Also write down what helped you feel better (if anything). Look back over your log to see if there are any patterns — do you always freak out right before a test? Do Mondays make you miserable? Figure out ways to head off the stress before it happens next time — work on a study system and get a good night's sleep before your next test, or treat yourself on Mondays with an extra-yummy breakfast.

✂ *LINKS*
To learn about how you can write your stress out in a journal, grab *Creativity* and turn to Chapter 3 (Write On!).

✸ *WORK IT!* Grab those images you made of yourself feeling tense and peaceful (in the exercise on page 127). Next to the wound-up image, write a list of things that make you feel that way. Next to the peaceful image, write a list of things that make you feel *that* way. Display them in your bedroom or paste them in your journal to remind yourself of what you can do to balance yourself.

> **✂ *LINKS***
> Chapter 6 (Feeling Healthy) has more on how to take care of your feelings and keep them balanced.

4. **Decide what's important to you and what's not.** In other words, what things are you worrying about that you might be able to let go of? Sure, you could freak about things like your shoelace breaking or a bad hair day, but are those things really that important in the big picture of the whole you?

✓ *REALITY CHECK* "I think I used to be more stressed out in elementary school than in middle school," says Hannah. "I used to focus a lot on what I was wearing or how my hair looked. But now that I have a more carefree attitude, every-thing is easier. I don't get upset as often and I've learned that one bad grade or one bad school picture isn't going to ruin the rest of my life."

WORK IT! Ask your parents, teachers, or other adults what kinds of things they stressed out about when they were your age. Do they still stress out about those things? Are there other things that they used to worry about but don't worry about anymore? What made them change?

*Answer to the allowance brain bender: You will have more than $100 in seven weeks. You'll have more than $1,000 in ten weeks (just three weeks later!).

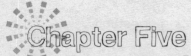

Chapter Five

Feeling Healthy

Feelings matter

The way you feel is just as important as how your body works in terms of keeping the whole you running right. No matter how healthy your body is, if your soul feels sick — like if you feel bad about yourself, or if you get angry a lot — then the whole you isn't doing so hot. If you feel bad a lot, or if you haven't learned how to handle difficult emotions, that can take a toll on your body, too. Your crummy feelings might prevent you from taking good care of yourself, or they might actually show up as physical symptoms.

> "Your emotions affect every cell in your body. Mind and body, mental and physical, are intertwined."
> — Thomas Tutko, psychologist

✔ *REALITY CHECK* "When I get very, very upset I get bad stomach- and headaches," says Courtney. "They don't go away until I calm myself down."

"I used to get so grumpy and mad all the time," says Mallory. "I would drown my emotions by eating constantly, usually sweets."

On the other hand, if you generally feel happy and even-keeled, it can do lots for your overall health. In this chapter, we'll explore your changing feelings and ways that you can keep healthy from an emotional point of view.

LINKS
Eating right, exercising, and generally taking good care of your body can make you feel good, too. For more on keeping your body in top shape, check out Chapter 2 (Eat Up!) and Chapter 3 (Working It).

You already know that your feelings are connected to your body somehow — maybe you've experienced joy (or anger or sadness) as an actual physical feeling. Emotions are also hugely affected by the chemicals sloshing around in your brain. So as you get older, your feelings change and become more intense as your body's hormones change. That's why it's so good to have ways to keep yourself balanced — so you can deal with these emotions when they happen.

✓ *REALITY CHECK* "As I've gotten older, I've found that I get mad a lot more easily and I tend to blow up at people a lot more," says Heidi.

"But I'm not sure if that is more from me growing up or just because my friends have gotten more annoying!"

⚓ *LINKS*
Flip back to Chapter 1 (Discovering Your Body) for more on the changes in your body. Turn to *Spirit,* **Chapter 1 ("Who Am I?"),** to read more about how the whole you is changing.

Your emotional diet

Just like you eat certain things to keep your body healthy and learn about certain things in school to keep your brain going strong, it's good to explore different ways to keep yourself *emotionally* healthy, too.

Being "emotionally healthy" doesn't mean that you're happy all the time — that's impossible. (It would be pretty annoying to be around, too!) It just means that you know how to deal with your feelings in a positive, balanced way. You don't focus on feeling bad 24/7, but you also deal with bad feelings when they happen and don't push them away as if they don't exist.

As you explore different strategies for staying emotionally healthy, you'll figure out what combination of things works best for *you* — that's what I call your *personal emotional diet.* Everyone's ideal emotional diet is slightly different, depending on who you are and

133

how you react to things. Some people like to work things out on their own; others like to talk it out with friends. Some people express their feelings through the arts; others like to work them out by exercising or playing sports. No matter what your style of dealing is, there are a few basic things that are good to have in your life to help you maintain balance:

- **Someone to talk to.** A friend, relative, teacher, counselor — anyone who will listen to you spill your guts without judging you. Even if you're the kind of person who'd rather work things out on your own, it feels good to know that you have someone you can turn to if you want to — and not just in bad times. It's also great to have someone you can share the good stuff with, too.

Did you know? People who have lots of different kinds of friends get sick less often — the theory is that having emotional support keeps you healthy!

✔ ***REALITY CHECK*** "When I was in seventh grade, I just started thinking I was a horrible person, I don't know why," says Gretchen. "I didn't say anything to anyone except my sixth-grade social studies teacher. She was like my guardian angel. Anytime I needed to talk to her, she was always there. She helped me through so much. Later I started talking to my minister, and she helped me take care of myself, too."

"WRITE IT!" List three people who you think you could talk to if you had a problem. List one friend your age, one relative (like your mom or dad, a sibling, a cousin, or an aunt or uncle), and one older person who's not a relative (like a teacher, coach, religious leader, or counselor). (If you don't have someone in one of those categories, can you think of any people who you'd like to be able to talk to if you knew them better?)

Friend: _____

Relative: _____

Other adult: _____

"WORK IT!" Make a mentor. A *mentor* is an older person who gives you advice, support, and guidance in your life. Sometimes finding a

135

mentor comes naturally, like when your coach is really cool and easy to talk to or when you have a favorite aunt whom you can tell *everything*. But if you don't have a ready-made mentor, you can develop one.

Pick an adult (who's not your mom or dad) whom you'd like to get to know better, someone whom you admire and you already have a friendly, positive relationship with — a teacher, an aunt or uncle, a coach. To get started, you could ask the adult if you could talk to her sometime about what she was like at your age. Ask her if she could give you some advice (about little things, to start with). As time goes on, you'll find it easier and easier to talk to her. You can also find a mentor through the Big Brothers Big Sisters of America (contact them at *http://www. bbbsa.org/*).

✂*LINKS*
Turn to *Friends and Family* for more on strengthening your relationships with the older people in your life.

- **A personal outlet.** Besides talking to someone else, it's good to have something that you can do on your own that helps you explore what you're going through, blow off icky feelings, or simply distract yourself. You could try writing in a journal, playing or listening to music, running, taking a walk, or anything that helps keeps you sane and level-headed.

%*LINKS*
Go to *Spirit,* Chapter 3 (The Way You Feel), for more ways to work through your feelings. *Creativity* has lots of creative outlets you can use. *Spirit,* Chapter 6 (Peace Out!), has more on ways to fill yourself up with peace and calm.

Even when you're not feeling bad, it's nice to make time for things you enjoy doing that are just for you. Doing stuff you love (whether that means shopping, painting, playing soccer, cooking, working on your Web site, playing video games, writing poetry, or anything else) keeps you balanced and happy.

✓ ***REALITY CHECK*** "When I feel upset or sad, I wait until I get home, then I write in my notebook about the emotions I'm feeling and I draw whatever pops into my head at the time," explains Heather. "Actually, I usually do that every night anyway, whether I feel upset or not."

"I go for walks a lot, and sometimes I run," says Jody. "I also write poems and songs in a journal that no one sees but me."

"When I get sad or upset, I dance," says Blair. "Even if I don't have dance class that day, I just dance on my own. It makes me feel better and gives me confidence."

"A lot of the time I'll go up to my room, turn my music on loud, and write in my journal," says Caitlin. "Other times, I'll turn my music on and just kind of look out the window. I have a great view of the mountains, so I can just sit on my bed and stare out the window. It's very peaceful. But if I'm really ticked, sometimes I'll vent my anger on one of my pillows until I feel better!"

►°WRITE IT!° What do you when you feel upset?

_____

_____

_____

►°WRITE IT!° List twenty things that you enjoy doing (like eating chocolate, listening to your favorite band, going hiking, reading a book, watching a basketball game, bowling, making grilled cheese sandwiches, etc.).

_____   _____

_____   _____

_____   _____

_____   _____

_____   _____

_____   _____

_____   _____

_____   _____

_____   _____

For the next two weeks, do something from this list every single day.

- **An idea of what makes you happy and sad.** And mad, and embarrassed, and hopeful, and afraid, and stressed . . . You get the idea. By learning how life's events tend to make you feel, you're less likely to feel overwhelmed by sudden, unexpected rushes of emotions. It's also good to have a general sense of what different emotions feel like — can you tell the difference between when you're tired and when you're feeling sad?

✄ ***LINKS***
**Read more
about the kinds
of journals you
can keep in**
Creativity,
**Chapter 3
(Write On!). To
learn more
about identify-
ing all your
emotions, turn
to** *Spirit,*
**Chapter 3 (The
Way You Feel).**

WRITE IT! Keep an emotional "weather report" journal. Every day, write about the emotions you had that day — happy, sad, whatever. (Use colors or images if that's easier for you.) If you can, try to note what it was that made you feel that way. By doing this, you can start to get an idea of what pushes your buttons. You can also use it to help you recognize what you're feeling and deal with it.

Working through it

Really intense feelings can throw you off balance, especially when they're not-so-great feelings, like sadness or anger. When you feel really bad, it's helpful to have a way of working out exactly why you feel that way and how to fix it. That way you can rebalance yourself and start to feel better faster. Think of it as your personal detective method — by investigating what you're feeling and uncovering the causes, you can help prevent it from happening again, or at least help yourself handle it better next time.

Next time you feel bad about something, try asking yourself these questions. (It helps to write down your answers, maybe in a journal.)

1. **"What am I feeling?"** Give your feeling a name: sadness, anger, frustration, jealousy, whatever it is. You might be feeling more than one emotion at once. Naming them all helps you to deal with them.

> ✂❖***LINKS***
> **Go to** *Spirit*,
> **Chapter 3 (The Way You Feel),**
> **for more on naming your feelings.**

2. **"What happened to make me feel this way?"** Did something specific happen? Draw or write it out in detail. Go ahead and vent! Be harsh and angry if you want to; be sad and sorry for yourself if you want to.

3. **"Why did it make me feel this way?"** Here, you have to dig a little deeper. If you're jealous because your older sister won a dance competition, why *exactly* did that make you feel jealous? Is it because you want to be as good a

dancer as she is? Is it because she always wins everything and you wish you could, too? Is it because your parents are really proud of her and you wish they would pay attention to you, too? This is the hardest part, so you might have to think about it awhile.

4. **"What can I do to feel better about it?"** Sure, you might feel better if that snotty kid who made fun of you got a big zit on the tip of his nose, but you can't exactly make that happen — and even if you could, making *him* miserable wouldn't really help *you*. What is something *you* can do to feel better? If you feel angry and embarrassed because your teacher punished you for talking in class, and you feel that way because you think she unfairly singled you out, will it make you feel better to talk to her about it? Will it make you feel better to run around the block a few times to blow off steam? Or will you feel better just by venting about it to your mom or a friend or in your journal? If that kid makes fun of you, will it make you feel better to talk to your friends? Or would you rather draw a picture of him with a big zit on his nose (to make yourself laugh)?

This is where figuring out *exactly* why you feel bad is a big help. So, using the example in #3, if you're jealous because your sister always wins everything, maybe it will make you feel better to think of things that *you* do well — even make a list of them! Or if you're jealous because your parents are paying so much attention to her, maybe

> **"Holding on to anger is like grasping a hot coal with the intent of throwing it at someone else; you are the one who gets burned."**
> **— Buddha, religious teacher and founder of Buddhism**

you'll feel better if you talk to them about it.

By working through those tough feelings and developing your own emotional diet, you'll be better prepared to deal with any difficulties that come your way. You'll also have a stronger foundation to start from when you encounter all the new and different feelings you'll experience in your life!

When bad moods don't go away

Sometimes a bad mood is more than just a bad mood. If you have feelings of sadness that last more than a couple of weeks, if you feel crabby or angry all the time, if you feel really hopeless or worthless, or if you ever feel so bad that you're considering hurting yourself, you may be depressed.

> ✓ ***REALITY CHECK*** "It's like a dark hole that you fell in and there's no ladder to climb out" is how Gretchen describes seriously low feelings.

Depression may feel inescapable, but it's possible and important to get help. If you or one of your friends just can't seem to get out of a slump, talk to your parents or another adult you trust right away. You can also call the **Girls and Boys Town National Hotline at 800-448-3000,** where you can talk to a professional counselor twenty-four hours a day about *any* problem. They can also refer you to resources in your area. Check out their Web site at *http://www.girlsandboys town.org/home.htm.*

If you want to learn more, the **National Institute of Mental Health** has an online brochure called "Let's Talk About Depression." It explains what depression is, and how to tell if you or someone you know is depressed. You can find it at *http://www.nimh.nih.gov/ publicat/letstalk.cfm.*

Conclusion

It's Up to You

Making your own choices

One of the coolest things about getting older is that you get to be more and more independent. You're starting to make your own choices about food, exercise, sleep, friends, school, and more. So just like it's helpful to explore different aspects of your creativity and your self, it's good to delve into all the options out there for keeping your mind and body at their best. The more you know, the better you'll be at making choices that really work for *you*.

For the rest of your life, you'll keep learning about your mind and body and doing different things to make them stronger and healthier. *You* get to decide how you want to get there. Why not start today?

WRITE IT! What's one thing you can do *today* to help your body or mind? (Flip back through the exercises in this book if you're having trouble thinking of something.) It can be as big or as small as you want.

_____

_____

Now do it!

"The root of
all health is in
the brain.
The trunk of it
is in emotion.
The branches
and leaves
are the body.
The flower of
health blooms
when all
parts work
together."
— Kurdish folk
wisdom

Getting into the habit of exploring and taking care of your body isn't just good for you now, it helps you get in the groove of having a healthier life, *all* your life. When you discover how to make eating exciting, have fun being active, and be good to your brain, you're making positive changes that will stay with you for years and years. The reward? A happier, healthier WHOLE YOU.

Appendix A
Learn More

If you'd like to learn more about some of the topics in this book, check out some of these books and Web sites. (Don't forget, though, information you get from a book or a Web site should never substitute for health advice from a real doctor. If you have any burning questions about your body or want to try a new exercise routine or food plan, ask your doc first, okay?)

Discovering your body

Eyewitness: Human Body, by Steve Parker (Dorling Kindersley, 2000) — All the body's systems and parts explained, with lots and lots of illustrations.

Growing Up: It's a Girl Thing, by Mavis Jukes (Knopf, 1998)

The What's Happening to My Body? Book for Girls and *The What's Happening to My Body? Book for Boys,* both by Lynda Madaras (Newmarket Press, 2000)

KidsHealth (*http://www.kidshealth.org/*) is a Web site for kids *and* parents. There's lots of information about health and your body, with special sections for parents, kids, and teens. Everything on the site is reviewed by doctors and other kids' health professionals.

The Yuckiest Site on the Internet (*http://yucky.kids.discovery.com*) has info on all kinds of silly, gross stuff about your body — click on "gross & cool body."

Eat up!

The Fannie Farmer Junior Cookbook, by Joan Scobey (Little Brown & Co., 2000)

Food Rules! The Stuff You Munch, Its Crunch, Its Punch, and Why You Sometimes Lose Your Lunch, by Bill Haduch (Puffin Books, 2001) — Detailed info on what you should eat and why, how to read a nutrition label, why certain foods make you fart, and more.

It's Disgusting and We Ate It! True Food Facts from Around the World and Throughout History, by James Solheim (Simon & Schuster, 1998) — Weird, gross things we humans eat (including some things you've eaten yourself!).

Kids Around the World Cook! The Best Foods and Recipes from Many Lands, by Arlette N. Braman (John Wiley & Sons, 2000) — This book talks about the history of different foods from around the world and includes really easy recipes.

The Sleepover Cookbook, by Hallie Warshaw (Sterling, 2000)

Epicurious (*http://eat.epicurious.com/*) has a searchable database of thousands of recipes, rated by people who've tried them.

A Teen's Guide to Going Vegetarian, by Judy Krizmanic (Puffin, 1994) — Detailed info on the benefits of going veggie, how to do it, dealing with people who don't get it, and more. Includes resources for getting active in environmental and animal rights issues.

The Teen's Vegetarian Cookbook, by Judy Krizmanic (Puffin, 1999)

Vegetables Rock! A Complete Guide for Teenage Vegetarians, by Stephanie Pierson (Bantam Doubleday Dell, 1999) — Written by a mom who decided to learn about vegetarianism when her daughter went veggie.

Working it

Eyewitness: Olympics, by Chris Oxlade and David Ballheimer (Dorling Kindersley, 2000)

Movin' and Groovin', by Peggy Buchanan and Linda Schwartz (The Learning Works, Inc., 1997) — Exercises you can do in your bedroom, in the kitchen, in your yard, out in the park, even on an airplane, with no equipment other than stuff you have lying around the house.

Teenage Fitness: Get Fit, Look Good, and Feel Great!, by Kathy Kaehler with Connie Church (HarperCollins, 2001) — Nutrition tips, workouts, and other get-fit advice. It's geared toward teen girls, but guys can use the info too.

Lives of the Athletes: Thrills, Spills (and What the Neighbors Thought), by Kathleen Krull and Kathryn

Hewitt (Harcourt Brace & Company, 1997) — Brief biographies of twenty history-making athletes, like Gertrude Ederle, who as a teenager became the first woman to swim across the English Channel.

Feed your brain

These books and Web sites have more brain benders for you to try:

Mensa Presents Mind Games for Kids (Barnes & Noble Books, 1997)

Games Magazine Presents the Kids' Giant Book of Games, edited by Karen C. Anderson (Random House, 1993)

FunBrain.com (*http://www.funbrain.com/kidscenter.html*)

NIEHS Kids' Pages (*http://www.niehs.nih.gov/kids/braint.htm*)

Recommended Reading

Looking for a good read? Check out some of the books listed here. They all relate to stuff that's in this book. I've recommended books for all different ages and reading levels, so ask your teacher or librarian if you're not sure about any of them.

S.O.R. Losers, by Avi

Tangerine, by Edward Bloor

Then Again, Maybe I Won't, by Judy Blume

The Moves Make the Man, by Bruce Brooks

Windmill Windup, by Matt Christopher

Whale Talk, by Chris Crutcher

The Snake-Stone, by Berlie Doherty

Orp and the Chop Suey Burgers, by Suzy Kline

The View from Saturday, by E.L. Konigsburg

On Different Shores, by Jen McVeity

The Grooming of Alice, by Phyllis Reynolds Naylor

Skinny-Bones, by Barbara Park

How to Eat Fried Worms, by Thomas Rockwell

Alphabet City Ballet, by Erika Tamar

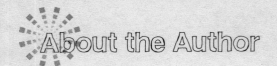

Jeannie Kim loves to swim but can't hit a tennis ball to save her life. A former editor at *YM* and *Twist,* she is now a full-time writer. Her work has appeared in *CosmoGIRL!* and *Your Prom,* as well as many magazines for grown-ups. She frequently writes about health, fitness, and nutrition. She's also played violin onstage at places like Boston's Symphony Hall and New York's CBGB (aka the birthplace of punk). She lives in New York City with her husband and their cat, Deirdre.